Native Americans

VOLUME 6

MANGAS COLORADAS–
MUSKOGEAN SPEAKERS

GROLIER

About this book

Thousands of years ago groups of hunter-gatherers from Asia began crossing the Bering Strait land bridge, which temporarily linked Siberia and Alaska. These earliest American settlers found a land of extreme environmental contrasts. Over the centuries the groups—ancestors of Native Americans—settled throughout North and South America, forming tribes and creating cultures and lifestyles that were influenced by their local environment. As in all parts of the world, conflicts emerged between the different tribes, but it was not until the arrival of Europeans in the late 15th and early 16th centuries that the survival of all Native Americans began to be threatened. Warfare, disease, and first European then American expansion combined to rid Native Americans of their homeland and, in most cases, their way of life. In the process whole tribes were wiped out, but many have survived. And for those that have, modern life has brought new challenges, cultural and political, that nonnative Americans are beginning to be made aware of.

There are 10 volumes in this set profiling all of the major Native-American groups, the history of their lives in each region, and background anthropology, archaeology, and other topics key to understanding Native Americans. Each volume contains entries ranging from important Native-American events and figures to wide-ranging beliefs and customs, an A–Z of some 90 tribes, and an index that covers the whole set. Also, each entry is fully illustrated with pictures, photographs, or maps and concludes with a list of cross-references to other entries in the set. This means readers can refer to each volume as a series of stories or cross-reference from one volume to another, following a subject that particularly interests them.

Published 2000 by Grolier Educational
Sherman Turnpike
Danbury, Connecticut 06816

Reprinted in 2001

© 2000 Brown Partworks Ltd

Set ISBN: 0-7172-9395-5
Volume ISBN: 0-7172-9401-3

Cover picture: Peter Newark Historical Pictures

For information address the publisher:
Grolier Educational, Sherman Turnpike,
Danbury, Connecticut 06816

Library of Congress Cataloging-in-Publication Data
Native Americans
p.cm.—Includes index.—Contents: v.1. Acoma–basketry—v.2. Bat cave–children—v.3. Chinook–education—v.4. El Tajín–Huron—v.5. Indian claims commission–longhouse religion—v.6. Mangas Coloradas–Muskogean speakers—v.7. Naskapi–Pontiac's war—v.8. Population density–Sauk and Fox—v.9. Scalping–tobacco—v.10. Toltec–Zuni.
1. Indians of North America Encyclopedia. Juvenile. [1. Indians of North America Encyclopedia.]
E76.2.N375 1999   99-28319
970.004'97'003—dc21   CIP

For Brown Partworks Ltd
CONSULTANT: Norman Bancroft Hunt
MANAGING EDITOR: Dawn Titmus
PROJECT EDITOR: Lee Stacy
ART DIRECTOR: Bradley Davis
DESIGNER: Paul Griffin
TEXT EDITORS: Robert Dimery, Peter Harrison,
    Lol Henderson, and Patrick Newman
PICTURE RESEARCH: Susannah Jayes and Rebecca Watson
INDEX: Kay Ollerenshaw
MAPS: William Lebihan

Printed in Singapore

CONTENTS

Mangas Coloradas

Born about 1791, Mangas Coloradas (Spanish for "red sleeves") grew up to become a warrior who was the scourge of white settlers in New Mexico and Arizona. A leader of the Mimbreno Apache, he had strong family connections with other Apache tribes, especially the Chiricahua: Cochise, the Chiricahua chief, was his son-in-law.

At first, Mangas Coloradas enjoyed good relations with white people, but the bitter struggle between the Apache and the Mexicans, and the greed of American miners, changed this.

In 1837, seeking the bounty offered by Mexico for Apache scalps, a group of miners invited some Apache to a dinner and murdered them.

Mangas Coloradas retaliated with a series of devastating raids on miners and settlers but still hoped to make peace. In 1846 and 1852 he signed treaties with the Americans, but his people were not treated fairly. The final straw came in 1852 when he made a friendly visit to miners at Palos Altos in southwestern New Mexico. They tied him up and whipped him.

REIGN OF TERROR

Apache raids under Mangas Coloradas followed throughout the 1850s, becoming especially intense after 1858, when the new Butterfield Overland Mail route started through Apache lands. In 1861 he joined forces with Cochise in a reign of terror. Together they controlled large parts of Arizona and New Mexico and blocked the

LEFT: Controlling canyon passes such as the Apache Trail pictured here, Mangas Coloradas was able to thwart the advances of white settlers and the U.S. Army into the Southwest.

Apache Pass to the west. Mangas Coloradas suffered a severe chest wound in a fight with soldiers at the pass. He survived but was tricked into being captured in January 1863. While under a flag of truce with the California Volunteers, he was meant to be discussing terms for ending the raids when they seized him.

The official army report said that Mangas Coloradas was then "shot [dead] while attempting to escape." In fact, he was shot on the orders of General Joseph West after being tortured with red-hot bayonets.

SEE ALSO:
❖ Apache
❖ Bows and Arrows
❖ Cochise
❖ Indian Wars
❖ Scalping
❖ Settlers
❖ Shields
❖ Warriors

Manifest Destiny

Many white Americans in the 19th century believed it was their God-given right and duty to expand their territories westward to the Pacific and beyond: it was their manifest, or obvious, destiny.

This idea was used by the U.S. government to justify campaigns against Native Americans and excuse the annexation (taking over) of the territories of Oregon, Texas, California, and New Mexico in the 1840s and 1850s. It was later used to justify U.S. involvement in Cuba, the Dominican Republic, Hawaii, Alaska, and the Philippines.

The term was first used in 1845, when editor John L. O'Sullivan prophesied "the fulfillment of our manifest destiny to overspread the continent allotted by Providence…" in his *United States Magazine and Democratic Review*. In other words, America was a gift from God, and its control by white Americans was inevitable. Following O'Sullivan's article, politicians quickly picked up on the term and used it regularly in debates on territorial matters.

THE MARCH OF "PROGRESS"

O'Sullivan and other white Americans believed God gave America to them because they were the most advanced and civilized people in the world—in human history, in fact. Their spread into new lands therefore represented "progress."

In turn, they considered that all Native Americans were inferior people with no right to the land under God's plan. Native Americans were exaggeratedly portrayed in newspapers—in both pictures and words—as violent savages who needed civilizing. This helped win white support for government campaigns against them.

RIGHT: This painting depicts settlers on the Oregon Trail in the 1860s.

SEE ALSO:
❖ Allotment Act
❖ Bureau of Indian Affairs
❖ Cattle Trails
❖ Disenfranchisement
❖ Indian Claims Commission
❖ Indian Territory
❖ Land Rights
❖ Settlers
❖ Wagon Trails

Marriage

Traditional Native-American marriages often appeared strange to Western eyes, since they were not bound by Christian conventions and rules. For all Native-American peoples marriage was a bond between two extended families as well as between two individuals. For the Cheyenne and Arapaho a marriage was the single most important event in a person's life, involving almost all the close relatives of the couple.

Because of their significance traditional Native-American marriages were subject to strict rules. The most important rule was that blood relatives, even quite distant ones, were not allowed to marry. This rule was often extended to include persons who were not related by blood but who belonged to the same clan or to a related clan. Among the Tlingit marriage was forbidden to anyone, even to members of other tribes, who claimed descent from the same mythical ancestor.

THE IMPORTANCE OF VIRTUE

Such restrictions meant that often prospective marriage partners could meet only at annual gatherings, when several families and clans camped together for tribal ceremonies. At such times young, sexually mature women were closely chaperoned, since among most tribes it was essential they remain chaste until marriage. A woman who respected her parents and remained virtuous would be sought as a wife; one who did not would lose respect.

A marriage was usually arranged by the relatives of the prospective bride and groom. A woman's brother often had the privilege of deciding whom she might marry, but this did not mean she had no say in the matter. In fact, it was usual to take a couple's preferences into account, for it was believed that forced marriages were unlikely to last or be happy.

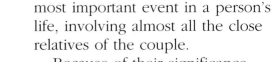

BELOW: Kiowa couples, such as this pair photographed in the late 1800s, lived with the husband's family.

LEFT: This young Hopi woman, photographed about 1900, is having her hair dressed in the traditional butterfly style to show she is sexually mature and therefore of marriageable age.

Parents were always concerned that their children should marry well, within their own class and to someone of similar status—although there were exceptions to this last rule—and that the marriage should be an honorable one. Elopements sometimes occurred—young couples secretly left a camp to live together. Such relationships did not have the blessing or approval of arranged marriages, but if they proved stable, they were generally accepted, and the couples lost no status or respect.

In many Native-American tribes a man could not marry until he had proved himself. For example, a Micmac man could not marry until he had spent up to two years living and working with his prospective father-in-law. During this time he had to prove his skills as a provider and hunter. Similarly, a Comanche man had to prove himself as a hunter and a warrior before he could marry. For this reason few Native-American men married until they were in their twenties, while most Native-American women could marry as soon as they were sexually mature.

In the case of an arranged marriage relatives of the man or woman—after lengthy family discussion—sent a representative to the other family with gifts. Which family made the first move varied

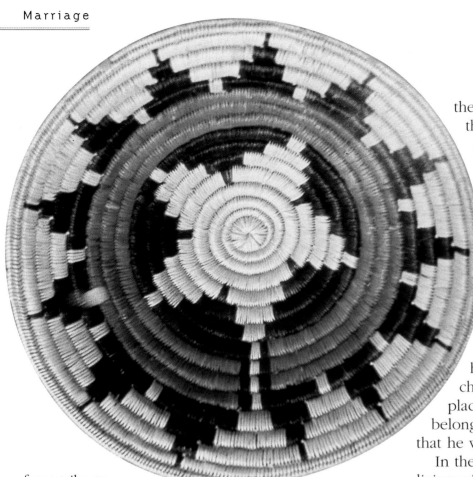

ABOVE: At Navajo weddings corn was given to the couple on a woven plaque such as this.

from tribe to tribe, but it was usually the man's. The family representative made a speech extolling the man's virtues, and if the gifts were accepted, then the marriage arrangements went ahead.

EXCHANGE OF GIFTS

Most families thought of the gifts— horses and weapons for the men, clothing, robes and drygoods for the women—as an honorable demonstration of the man's potential as a provider and not as an attempt to "buy" a wife. Later, gifts of equal or greater value would be given by the woman's relatives in honor of their own family name. Exchanging gifts this way forged a bond between the families and validated the marriage.

The young Native-American couple then started living together as husband and wife with one of

the families. If they lived with the wife's family, it was the son-in-law's responsibility to care and provide for his wife's older relatives. Marriages and the family ties they established were intended to last, but couples could divorce simply if they wanted to. In the case of a couple living with the wife's family, the woman owned all the household items and when choosing to end the marriage placed her husband's few belongings outside to indicate that he was no longer welcome.

In the case of a married couple living with the husband's family, the wife simply packed up and returned to her family. He, in turn, could reject her, if she proved unfaithful or lazy, by sending her back to her relatives or returning to his own family. In nearly all cases of divorce young children remained with their mother.

In some Native-American tribes, such as the Comanche, polygamy— a man having more than one wife—was common. Usually, however, a man could marry only as many wives as he could afford to provide for. For this reason polygamy was practiced mainly by tribal chiefs and other rich men. In such cases the man normally married his first wife's sisters, cousins, or nieces.

In most Native-American tribes, however, marriage between two people was intended to last for the rest of their lives.

SEE ALSO:
- ❖ Arapaho
- ❖ Birth Customs
- ❖ Cheyenne
- ❖ Children
- ❖ Clan
- ❖ Comanche
- ❖ Homes
- ❖ Hopi
- ❖ Kiowa
- ❖ Micmac
- ❖ Navajo
- ❖ Ritual
- ❖ Tlingit
- ❖ Women

Martinez, Maria

ABOVE: Even after becoming famous worldwide, Maria lived and worked in the village where she was born.

Maria Martinez is the most celebrated 20th-century ceramic artist of the Pueblo people of the southwestern United States. She is justly famous worldwide for the outstanding quality of her pottery, which she based on traditional Pueblo styles.

Maria Martinez was born in the Tewa village of San Ildefonso in northern New Mexico. The exact date of her birth is uncertain, but it is known that she was baptized in 1887, so she was probably born about 1884. She began making pottery in 1897, when she was only about 13 years old.

INTRIGUING DISCOVERY

In 1908 Dr. Edgar Lee Hewett, an archaeologist from the Museum of New Mexico, began excavating an abandoned Tewa village in the Frijoles Canyon, near San Ildefonso. He grew curious about some thin and unusually black shards of pottery that he discovered at the site. Local people recommended he show them to Maria, who by then was renowned for her skill at making thin, shapely pottery using the local clay, which was notoriously difficult to work with.

Maria successfully copied the shards but at first failed to reproduce their exact coloring. So she began experimenting, with the help of her husband, Julian. Eventually, they discovered how to duplicate the pots exactly. Pottery is hardened by firing it—heating it in a fire—twice. Maria and Julian found that by smothering the flames with animal dung at the second firing, the smoke from the burning dung

gave their ware the same beautiful black sheen as the shards. Dr. Hewett alerted overseas collectors, and Maria and Julian quickly gained an international reputation.

Maria Martinez was subsequently invited to lay the cornerstone of Rockefeller Center in New York in honor of her achievements. She continued to work after Julian's death in 1943 and always readily shared her knowledge with fellow potters in San Ildefonso.

Maria Martinez died in 1980, but her fabulous Pueblo pots live on in museums and private collections around the world.

SEE ALSO:
- ❖ Art
- ❖ Pottery
- ❖ Pueblo
- ❖ Southwest

Masks

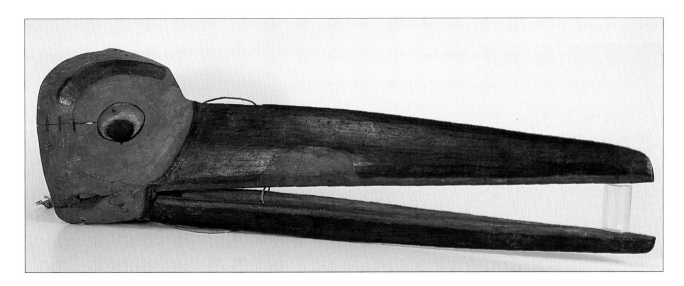

Many Native Americans used masks in their religious rituals and ceremonies. They were made from a variety of different materials, including wood, leather, and vegetable fibers, and were often painted with designs representing the spirit or ancestor associated with the mask. Many of them were made for specific tribal rituals or ceremonies, during which the presence of the mask played an essential role and symbolized the connection between the human and spirit worlds.

A LINK TO THE SPIRIT WORLD

In traditional Native-American cultures the spirit world is as real as the natural world. Masks served to provide a link between these two worlds and also reminded the tribespeople that the supernatural beings were available to give them help and assistance. Many of these connections are explained in tribal stories and legends, which were told during the winter months.

Different tribes used masks in different ways. For example, the Iroquois tribe members who wore Husk Faces went from longhouse to longhouse performing a dance that represented the return of the crops in the spring. Another example of masks being used in rituals to ask favors of the spirits was the Kachina Dance of the Hopi. This, too, was performed in the hope of a successful harvest.

The Kwakiutl used masks in their Hamatsa Dance to commemorate an important supernatural event in their folklore. The dance was an initiation ceremony for new members of their community. The dancer represented a tribal ancestor who changed from a human to a spirit and learned some of the dances of the spirit world. The ancestor then returned to the tribe, where more ritual dances made him human again. He then taught his fellow tribespeople the spirit dances he had learned.

MORE THAN JUST SYMBOLIC

During such rituals it was believed the performers did not just play the roles of the spirits depicted by their masks. The masks helped the

ABOVE: The beak and eyes of this painted cedar Kwakiutl raven mask are hinged so that the wearer can open and close them.

dancers actually become—for the duration of the dance—the spirits that they were portraying.

For example, when a group of Hopi villagers watched the dance to celebrate the kachina (ancestral spirits), they believed that they were not just watching their masked neighbors perform a dance but were seeing them change before their very eyes into the kachina that made successful farming possible.

In this way the mask helped create a powerful social bond between people. If people believed their neighbor in some way played an important part in the successful growing of their crops, they were much more likely to treat him or her, and their community as a whole, with respect.

CARING FOR THE MASKS

Since masks were considered to be so important, great care went into making them. For example, the Iroquois mask carvers went into the forest to look for the right tree—preferably a basswood, cucumber, or willow tree. The carver worked into the tree, carving the face into the living wood. He then carefully removed the mask in one piece, then smoothed and polished the inside. If he carved the mask in the morning, he painted it red. If he carved it in the afternoon or evening, he painted it black.

Masks were usually stylized and always showed specific features. The False Face masks of the Iroquois all had twisted noses

BELOW: Made from seven pieces of jade, this mask was found at the site of the major Mayan city of Palenque in Mexico. It was used in burial rituals and dates from the Late Classic period, between A.D. 550 and A.D. 900.

because, according to legend, the giant False Face ran into a mountain and broke his nose.

The Haida people made masks of the Cannibal Spirit in two separate halves. At a specific point in the dance the two halves suddenly opened to reveal the face of the dancer, who represented a human prisoner of the spirit.

Native-American masks often belonged to specific ritual or religious groups and might be looked

after by people who had a special duty to care for them. In Pueblo communities, for example, the masks that were used in the dances to celebrate the kachina (ancestral spirits) were kept in the sacred ritual centers called *kivas*, where they were guarded by *kiva* priests.

Another example is the Iroquois, who covered their False Face masks with hide or cloth and hung them so that they faced the wall. In this way the power of the False

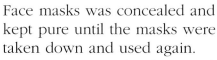

RIGHT: Fur from a grizzly bear adorns this mask of the Northwest Coast Bella Coola culture. It is said to show a human face, but the meaning of the horns is unknown.

LEFT: Decorated with feathers, this Inuit mask has only one eye-hole.

Face masks was concealed and kept pure until the masks were taken down and used again.

Sometimes masks also acquired other social meanings. On the Northwest Coast they were owned by individual families. Since some of the masks were used only in the more important tribal dances, they would show the status of the dancer and the dancer's family when they were worn.

SEE ALSO:
- ❖ Afterlife
- ❖ Dance
- ❖ Death Customs
- ❖ Featherwork
- ❖ Haida
- ❖ Hopi
- ❖ Inuit
- ❖ Iroquois
- ❖ Kachina
- ❖ Kiva
- ❖ Kwakiutl
- ❖ Longhouse
  Religion
- ❖ Maya
- ❖ Medicine
- ❖ Origin Myths
- ❖ Palenque
- ❖ Pueblo
- ❖ Ritual
- ❖ Shamanism

Maya

The Mayan civilization began as early as 1500 B.C. but declined long before Columbus arrived in the Americas in the late 15th century. It was a sophisticated civilization comparable to that of Ancient Greece, with beautiful architecture and artifacts, and advanced systems of astronomy and mathematics. Mayan glyphs, or picture-writings, tell scholars about the complex political and religious structure of Mayan society and how the Mayan empire rose and fell.

The Maya lived on the Yucatán Peninsula in Mexico and in neighboring areas. Their civilization extended to neighboring tribes, such as the Huastec and the Quiche. These tribes all lived in an area that scholars now refer to as Mesoamerica—that is, parts of present-day Mexico, Guatemala, Belize, Honduras, and Nicaragua.

Olmec inheritance

The Mayan tribes were descended from an earlier civilization, the Olmec. The Olmec are known today as the mother civilization of Mesoamerica. They are thought to have invented a system of writing and to have been among the first people to cultivate corn, a crop that

LEFT: At the height of their civilization the Maya built many imposing stone pyramids with temples on top. This one, in the city of Uxmal, is called the Pyramid of the Magician.

they developed over many centuries from wild grass seeds. The Mayan civilization was the greatest to emerge after the Olmec.

The Maya had a staple diet of corn but also grew crops that were unknown outside the Americas, such as tomatoes, chili peppers, pumpkins, avocados, peanuts, and beans. Because of their plentiful supply of food the Maya were able to spend time building great cities, which became centers of culture, learning, commerce, and religious ceremonies. There were more than 100 of these cities in Mesoamerica, each full of magnificent stone buildings, such as pyramids with temples on top, palaces, and vaulted tombs. The cities also had bridges, paved roads, bathhouses, courts for ball games, and squares.

Each city was like a state, with its own ruler. The citizens were divided into three social classes. First were the priests, who were called the Keepers of Knowledge. Next were the Sun Children, who administered taxes, commerce, and the law. Then came craftworkers such as potters, stoneworkers, and tailors. In the countryside around the cities lived the farmers, who usually had small, one-roomed houses made of adobe (bricks of straw and clay) and thatch—much like the houses their descendants live in today.

The Maya were skilled weavers and spinners, and also made fine pottery and silver, copper, shell, and feather jewelry. It seems that they did not use wheeled vehicles or metal tools, though.

MAIN MAYAN CITIES

During the Classic period, from about A.D. 300 to A.D. 900, Mayan civilization spread over a population of some 10 million. Great cities, such as Tikal, Uxmal, Becan, Chitchén Itzá, and Seibal, were built, and they became independent Mayan kingdom-states.

The greatest city was Palenque, known as the jewel of the Mayan world. In 1952 an archaeologist called Alberto Ruz found a huge tomb at the site of Palenque. Inside was a crypt that had been sealed for over 1,200 years. It contained the sarcophagus, or stone coffin, of

LEFT: The Maya were skillful potters who often painted their vessels with glyphs and pictures of gods and important people.

From Lord Pacal's coffin they found out that Mayan rulers had their pyramids built for them during their lifetimes, so that people could remember and worship them immediately after their deaths. This meant that the rulers thought of themselves as gods.

The archaeologists also discovered that the Maya worshiped many gods of nature. One of the most important was Chac, the god of rain. The Maya practiced many rituals to make sure that Chac sent

Palenque's most powerful ruler, Lord Pacal, whose name means Great Shield. Above Lord Pacal's head was a life-sized jade mask.

CRUCIAL BREAKTHROUGH

Not long after this great find archaeologists discovered how to decipher the glyphs carved on the coffin. For many years they had been trying to work out the meanings of glyphs inscribed on Mayan buildings and tombs. They had also found books, which were folded sheets of paper made from plant fibers. Finally, they worked out a series of codes that told them a great deal about Mayan civilization.

From the books archaeologists learned about topics such as agriculture, weather, medicine, and astronomy. They also found that the Maya had a highly accurate calendar.

ABOVE: The Maya decorated the walls of many buildings with plaster figures, such as this life-sized head found at the city of Palenque.

RIGHT: The figure on the front of this Mayan incense-burner, found at Palenque, may represent the Sun God. He is shown standing on a turtle from which the chief god of the underworld is emerging.

ABOVE: The glyphs on this Mayan stone beam depict animals, which represent periods of time, and gods, which represent numbers. Added together they mean February 11, A.D. 526, in the modern calendar.

which the players had to compete for their lives, and human heads were used instead of balls.

Nobody knows for sure what caused the decline of the Mayan civilization. Some scholars believe it was a combination of civil war and natural disasters such as drought. For hundreds of years after their decline the Mayan cities lay hidden in the jungle, until they were uncovered by Spanish explorers in the 16th century. Over the next few centuries the Spanish conquered most of the remaining Mayan tribespeople. But it was not until the early 1800s that the Mexican government subdued the last independent Mayan communities.

NEGLECTED PEOPLE

During the 19th century archaeologists became very interested in the relics of Mayan civilization. Sadly, there was less interest in the living descendants of the Maya. Today the few remaining Maya are mostly poor peasant farmers in Mexico, Guatemala, and Belize. They speak Mayan dialects and make traditional Mayan pottery and sculpture.

them plenty of rain for their crops. There was also a creator god, Kukulcan—who was similar to the Aztec god Quetzalcoatl—and Itzamina, a god of the sky. The Maya put complete trust in these gods, whom they believed controlled all aspects of their destiny.

One of the most interesting discoveries that archaeologists made was that far from being a peaceful people, as was once thought, the Maya were actually violent and aggressive. The Maya placed great value on the military conquest of other tribes and often performed cruel human sacrifices to their gods. In addition they held games in

Means, Russell

R ussell Means (born 1939) is an Oglala Sioux activist from the Pine Ridge reservation in South Dakota and a leader of the American Indian Movement (AIM).

AIM was founded in 1968 in Minneapolis as a radical, militant group to protect Native-American treaty rights and to stop alleged police harassment. Means has described it as the only truly revolutionary Native-American group in the United States.

UPHOLDING TRADITION
Although Means is often labeled a communist, this is not so. Fundamentally, he seeks a return to traditional Native-American customs. According to his philosophy, he

ABOVE: In 1983 Russell Means helped organize a Wounded Knee memorial, an event that included a three-day march.

rejects what he sees as the "European" addiction to material goods and seeks to restore people to their rightful place as spiritual beings in harmony with nature.

Means has a flair for daring and memorable publicity stunts. At the end of the Trail of Broken Treaties march from the West Coast in 1972 he organized the six-day occupation of the offices of the Bureau of Indian Affairs in Washington. The following year Wounded Knee was occupied by AIM for 71 days in commemoration of the infamous massacre there in 1890.

ATTRACTING ATTENTION
These actions highlighted the need for radical reforms in reservation administration and the renewal of old treaty rights, but Means has also been criticized for his confrontational style. The Wounded Knee protest led to a gun battle in which two Native Americans were killed by FBI agents.

More recently Means has attracted some criticism for appearing in Hollywood movies such as *Natural Born Killers* and *The Last of the Mohicans*. However, few people have done as much as he has since the 1960s to bring wide attention to Native-American issues.

SEE ALSO:
- Bureau of Indian Affairs
- Disenfranchisement
- Land Rights
- Legislation
- Movies
- Recognition
- Reservations
- Sacred Sites
- Sioux
- Wounded Knee

Medicine

Traditional Native-American medicine embraces a variety of activities besides dispensing potions for sickness and applying treatments for injury. These activities include clairvoyance, prophecy, divination, and states of ecstatic trance undergone by shamans (medicine men and women).

Native Americans believed that plants, animals, rocks, and all other natural phenomena possessed "power"—the ability to reason and to motivate or influence objects and events. It followed, therefore, that disease had one of three causes: human, natural, or supernatural.

CAUSE AND EFFECT

Anything with an obvious human or natural cause—such as a broken bone or a flesh wound—was treated with natural herbs and concoctions. Many of these remedies proved highly successful, and more than 200 natural Native-American drugs have appeared in the *Pharmacopoeia of the United States* since the publication of its first edition in 1820.

However, any sickness, disease, lethargy, or other ailment with no obvious human or natural cause was attributed to a mysterious, supernatural source.

MEDICINE AND MYSTERY

Medicine nearly always involved mystery. A shaman's power was mysterious because it came from the realm of the spirits and the supernatural. Cures were made through the intervention of the mysterious spirit sources with which a shaman was in contact.

RIGHT: Some Crow warriors wore an eagle's talon in the belief that its medicine power would help them strike down their enemies—just like an eagle striking down its prey.

A shaman used ritual formulas, equipment, language, and chants to make contact with the spirits.

Ritual played an essential role in all aspects of Native-American life, including war, art, and finding food. Ritual and medicine, or mystery, were linked with everyday practical matters in a way that made little distinction between the natural and the supernatural.

Native Americans had a reverent and holistic (all-embracing) view of the world, considering themselves part of nature. Magic and mystery were inseparable from practical science, and both were explained through the myths and legends that were conceived as a way of understanding reality.

Sacred objects, music, dance, and personal humility and sacrifice to gain favor with the spirits were part of everyday life for Native Americans. And through ritual and ceremony they related directly to the idea of medicine power as a mysterious force.

THE SOURCE OF ALL POWER

Many tribes believed this power came from a single and often unnameable and unknowable spirit source. The Algonquian groups knew this power as Manitou, the Iroquois called it Orenda, and the Sioux named it Wakonda. This power was the Great Medicine, or Great Mystery, or Mysterious One, from which everything, including people, derives motivation, reason, strength, and belief. It was the source of all power invested in people and in the spirits or ghosts of dead ancestors, in animals and

ABOVE: Personal medicine necklaces like this one were commonly worn by Plains tribespeople.

plants, and in natural phenomena such as the sun and rain. It was possessed in equal amounts by guardian spirits, such as the kachinas of the Southwest, and demons, like the Algonquian windigos believed to haunt the Subarctic wastelands.

To the European colonists—despite their own beliefs in a large number of saints and demons

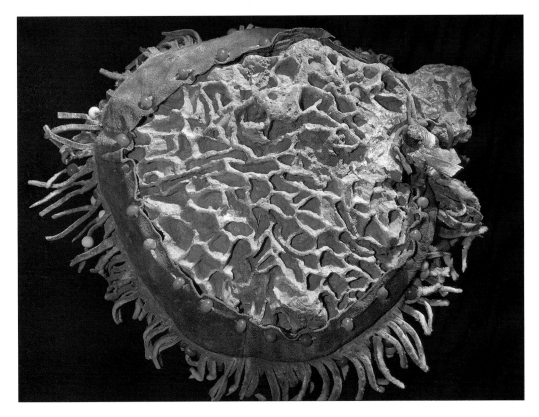

LEFT: Crow people wrapped rocks in buckskins adorned with beads and kept them in medicine bundles. These bundles were opened at the first sound of thunder in spring and again before the onset of winter. This was done during the Singing of the Cooked Meat ceremony to bring the Crow people good fortune.

possessing magical or miraculous powers—this was all superstitious paganism. Shamans were accordingly seen as the main barrier to wiping out Native-American culture and converting Native Americans to Christianity. The Spanish, French, and English not only sent armies to wage war, they sent missionaries to discredit the beliefs of the shamans.

DEFENDING THEIR BELIEFS

These attempts often met with strong resistance. The Pueblo Rebellion of 1680 was a response to brutal religious suppression, and the pan-Indian movements against colonialism led by Tecumseh, Pontiac, and Black Hawk in the late 18th and early 19th centuries were inspired by "prophets" preaching a return to the old medicine ways. Even the famous Sioux warrior,

Sitting Bull, and Geronimo, the famous Apache resistance leader, were shamans, not military leaders.

Today medicine power continues to be a source of strength for many Native Americans and is rapidly gaining a following among a broad cross-section of other people.

SEE ALSO:

- ❖ Algonquian
- ❖ Black Hawk's War
- ❖ Crow
- ❖ Dance
- ❖ Geronimo
- ❖ Iroquois
- ❖ Kachina
- ❖ Medicine Bundle
- ❖ Medicine Wheel
- ❖ Missions
- ❖ Music
- ❖ Plains
- ❖ Pueblo Rebellion
- ❖ Ritual
- ❖ Shamanism
- ❖ Sioux
- ❖ Sitting Bull
- ❖ Tecumseh
- ❖ Warriors

Medicine Bundle

ABOVE: Belonging to the weasel chapter of the Crow Tobacco society, this bundle was opened during ceremonies to insure a good crop. Women then danced wearing the weasel skins.

Medicine bundles were collections of objects normally kept in a pouch made from an animal or bird skin. The bundles acted as symbols linking the person who made or owned the bundle to the animal spirits who appeared in that person's vision, which gave him or her special power.

THE POWER OF THE BUNDLE

Native Americans believed in many gods and spirits. These spirits became visible to individuals during intense dreams or visions giving them power that could be used to do good and counteract evil. Such power could be used to cure an illness or bring a person good luck. The bundle could also bring the owner success in battle or in hunting as well as benefit the community as whole.

During the vision the animal spirit instructed the person having the vision to make a medicine bundle somehow associated with the animal. In other words, if a man dreamed of a beaver, then he would use a beaver skin for his bundle.

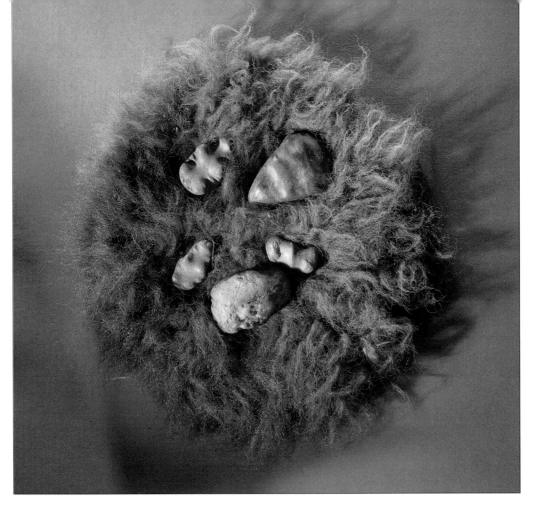

LEFT: This medicine bundle of strangely shaped stones wrapped in buffalo hair was used by Blackfoot people during rituals to call up buffalo in times of drought.

The bundles also contained other objects, such as rocks, beads, animal claws, or parts of plants. These were items that would link the owner to the spirit world but in a way only the owner would understand.

Anyone could own a medicine bundle, providing the person had had a vision explaining its use. Although the bundles themselves did not possess any power, they reminded their owners of the original visions or dreams and could therefore be used to reactivate them during ceremonies.

TRIBAL BUNDLES

Medicine bundles figured in mythical accounts of the past. The Navajo believed that a medicine bundle brought from the underworld was used by First Man and First Woman, in an all-night ceremony at the Place of Emergence, to set in place the "inner forms" of the natural world. This bundle was passed on to Changing Woman, who used it to create corn. Thus the power of a medicine bundle could start life itself.

Some bundles belonged to sacred societies. The bundle of a society often included an object that the society believed once belonged to an early ancestor. The Iroquois had eight ritual societies that used medicine bundles. The most powerful of them was the Little Water Medicine, which used a special potion made from water and animal parts with its bundles.

The Pawnee made bundles from animal hide, which they painted with patterns to represent stars. Sometimes they wrapped the hide around an ear of corn to unite the animal world with that of agriculture. The Pawnee were both hunters and farmers, and this helped insure a yearly supply of food.

SEE ALSO:
❖ Algonquian
❖ Blackfoot
❖ Crow
❖ Iroquois
❖ Longhouse
  Religion
❖ Medicine
❖ Medicine
  Wheel
❖ Navajo
❖ Pawnee
❖ Ritual
❖ Shamanism
❖ Sioux
❖ Tobacco

Medicine Wheel

The medicine wheel, or sacred circle, was a common Native-American symbol. It had many different meanings. In some places it was a sign for healing, but it could also be understood as a representation of the four seasons or the four stages of human life—childhood, adolescence, maturity, and old age. It was often painted on rocks and war shields. Giant medicine wheels were also marked out with stones on the tops of hills and mountains of the Great Plains.

A medicine wheel is a form of mandala, or circle, that represents the world and the surrounding forces of the universe. The outer circle symbolizes the edge of the world, while the spokes of the wheel cross the center and represent the sacred paths of the sun and of humanity. An altar at the center, which was sometimes marked with an eagle feather or a buffalo skull, stands for the power of the Creator. Four sacred colors, symbolizing various relationships among four things (such as the points of the compass), are often shown too.

RIGHT: Painted on rock, this small medicine wheel is in Bernalillo County in New Mexico.

MOUNTAIN WHEEL

The largest medicine wheel in the U.S. was built atop the west peak of Medicine Mountain in Bighorn National Forest, Wyoming. Made up of limestone slabs and boulders, it is 75 feet (23 m) wide and has a circumference of 245 feet (74 m). At the center is a circular mound 3 feet (1 m) high, which probably represents the sun. Radiating from this central mound are 28 long, narrow spokes, which may relate to the 28 days of the lunar month.

SEE ALSO:
- Art
- Buffalo
- Cosmology
- Fasting
- Homes
- Medicine
- Medicine Bundle
- Origin Myths
- Plains
- Ritual
- Sacred Sites
- Shamanism
- Shields
- Travois

Several low shelters were built at varying distances from the center. One was at the end of a long spoke beyond the rim, while another was at the end of a short spoke. These shelters probably were made of slabs of rock supported by heavy pine logs, the remains of some of which have been found among the stones. Only one of the shelters opens toward the center of the wheel.

The shelters may have represented the planets and their different positions in relation to the sun. They would have been used by chiefs or shamans (medicine men or women) from different tribes during ceremonies. Nobody knows exactly what took place at these ceremonies, but it is thought they included placing a bleached buffalo skull to face the rising sun.

The exact meaning of the medicine wheel at Bighorn is unknown. The Crow, who live in the area, say it is ancient but have no myths or legends to explain its origin. It is seen by them as a place of mystery, and trails worn by horses or dogs pulling travois (sledlike poles) suggest it was visited regularly.

Mesa Verde

Mesa Verde (which means "green table" in Spanish) is a series of 20 canyons containing the ruins of some 1,000 prehistoric cliff dwellings. It is near the Mancos River, in southwestern Colorado.

The canyons and mesa tops are about 20 miles (32 km) long and are surrounded by forests of juniper, spruce, cedar, and piñon. The area was named by Spanish Franciscan missionary Father Francisco Silvestre Escalante, who visited in 1776 while seeking a route from Santa Fe to Monterey. In 1906 the area was incorporated into a 50,000-acre (20,250-ha) national park.

The first inhabitants of Mesa Verde were probably Mongoloid hunters, who temporarily sheltered in the natural caves halfway up the sandstone cliffs about 12,000 years

BELOW: Spruce Tree House is the third largest cliff dwelling in Mesa Verde. It has 114 rooms, including some small storage spaces, and was built over the course of 100 years.

ago. Permanent settlement began with the Anasazi people from as early as 500 B.C. At first they lived in the caves, then later they moved to the relatively flat mesa tops, where they built pit houses covered by poles and adobe (clay and straw) mortar. These they gradually enlarged and joined together.

MOVING INTO THE CAVES

By about A.D. 1000 Mesa Verde was developing into a series of small villages along the mesa tops and surrounding valleys. During this time the Anasazi increasingly moved their villages into the caves, possibly for defensive reasons. From A.D. 950 onward the inhabitants built towers of two and three stories, possibly as observation posts. The cost, time, and energy

required to build a settlement in such an inaccessible location also indicate that its position was selected for defensive reasons.

FINGERPRINTS FROM THE PAST

The multistoried cliff dwellings were built using poles set into masonry walls, with floors built from smaller poles and willows overlaid with adobe. Sandstone was cut and shaped into blocks by crude stone axes and laid in adobe. Sometimes the walls were finished with plaster. Small fingerprints in the plaster suggest women played a major role in the building work.

The largest and best known cliff dwelling at Mesa Verde was Cliff Palace—a series of houses, plus a large round tower, in an arc about 300 feet (90 m) long.

The second largest ruin, Balcony House, is almost completely inaccessible and can be entered only along several narrow ledges. It contains a paved court, with two-story houses built on three sides and narrow balconies running along to the doorways of the upper levels. The rooms are rectangular and would have accommodated up to 40 people. Few of the rooms had windows. Doorways are rectangular or T-shaped (for some unknown reason) and would have been closed by placing a flat slab or rock against their openings.

UNFINISHED MYSTERY

Sun Temple is one of the most unusual sites. Stone tools were found in this unfinished building, which is 131 feet (40 m) long and built in a D shape, with three *kivas*—round, partly underground ceremonial structures. Its unusual features include its huge walls, which are 3 feet (1 m) deep and made of stone facings filled with earth. Archaeologists believe that the site was probably a ceremonial center since there is no evidence of people using it as a home.

SEE ALSO:
❖ Anasazi
❖ Canyon de Chelly
❖ Chaco Canyon
❖ Cliff Palace
❖ Kiva
❖ Missions
❖ Pueblo
❖ Southwest

Mestizos

LEFT: This painting from about 1775 shows a family made up of a Spanish-American woman, a Native-American man, and their mixed-race, Mestizo child.

The Mestizos were people with Spanish and Native-American ancestry—*mestizo* is Spanish for "mixed race." Few women accompanied the Spanish conquistadors of the 16th and 17th centuries on their trips to the Americas. The men planned to pillage gold, silver, and other riches, not settle down and raise families. However, those men who did stay often took mistresses from among the local people. One of the first Mestizos was Martin, the son of Hernando Cortés, conqueror of Mexico, and his Native-American interpreter, Malinche.

Mestizos were not fully accepted by either the Spanish or Native Americans. To the Spanish they were racially inferior and could never attain the status of full-blooded Europeans. To Native Americans they were people who simply did not fit into the traditional way of life.

With the addition of Africans, who the Spanish brought forcibly to the colonies as slaves, there were three separate races, as well as the various mixes—children with Spanish and African parents were called Mulattos, and those born to Native Americans and Africans, Zambos.

Unlike the Métis—their French and Native-American counterparts in the North—the Mestizos did not form a distinct group. They tended to live on the margins of Native-American society or were absorbed into the Spanish townships.

CULTURAL INHERITANCE

Today Spanish influence on tribes-people is seen more readily in customs than in blood lines. A good example is the *matachine* dances of the Yaqui and Pueblo tribes. In them Catholic Easter celebrations and tribal hunting rites mingle.

Métis

The Métis are a group of mixed-race people in Canada who are descended from late 17th-century Cree and French and Scottish fur trappers and traders—*métis* is French for "mixed race."

In the late 17th century trading companies such as the Hudson's Bay Company sent out fur trappers and traders to the unexplored areas of western North America. This was in response to the demands of the growing European middle class, which was beginning to develop a taste for luxury goods such as fur coats and hats. Over the next two centuries the demand for fur greatly increased—especially for beaver fur, which was used to adorn many fashionable clothes. As a result more and more trappers went out in search of beaver in areas such as Saskatchewan in Canada.

FRIENDLY RELATIONS

Europeans thought Saskatchewan was uninhabited; but when the first trappers and traders arrived, they found Cree tribespeople had been living there for centuries. They offered the Cree goods in return for their help as guides and hunters. The whites and the Cree befriended each other, lived side by side, and shared the same rugged life.

Young Frenchmen were actively encouraged to marry Cree women in the belief that this would help spread French culture and expand opportunities for trade. Over the

ABOVE: This 1885 photograph shows a Métis scout of the Northwest Mounted Police.

years many French and Scottish trappers married into Cree tribes and had children. These children, the first Métis, adopted aspects of both cultures: for example, they performed Native-American religious rituals while also practicing the Catholic faith. They continued to work as fur trappers and traders, and often acted as interpreters for negotiations between Cree and Europeans. The British Northwest Company, which competed with the French in the fur trade, was staffed mainly by Métis.

At the end of the 18th century, when the British ousted the French and white settlements became more fully established, the status of the Métis declined. Not being fully

ABOVE: *The Thirsty Trapper*, painted in 1850 by Alfred Miller, illustrates the friendliness that developed between Cree and Europeans.

Native Americans, they had no historical claims to owning land. Not being Europeans, they could not claim an automatic right to land. Some Métis were forced to leave their homes. In the 19th century more and more white settlers poured into the region as railroads were built. The Métis tried to protect their land and trapping and trading rights in the two Riel Rebellions (1869–1870 and 1885) but were eventually defeated.

STAKING THEIR CLAIM

The Métis have a major presence in Canada today. They are proud of their heritage and strive to maintain aspects of the unique culture of their Métis ancestors.

Their status has become an important political issue in Canada. For years the Métis have been ignored by successive governments while other Native-American peoples have had their claims heard. For this reason the Métis were once known as *ootip ayim sowak*, meaning "the people nobody knows."

Being of mixed-race descent, the Métis have had neither Native nor white American status. However, the number of societies battling for their rights and interests has grown considerably in recent years.

SEE ALSO:
- Cree
- Fur Trade
- Hudson's Bay Company
- Interpreters
- Mestizos
- Missions
- Railroads
- Riel Rebellions
- Settlers
- Trade
- Urban Life

Micmac

The Micmac lived in eastern Canada. They probably migrated from the Great Lakes region to what are now the Canadian maritime provinces long before Europeans arrived on the continent. Living on or near the coast, they developed their own unique culture from the traditional hunter-gatherer way of life characteristic of eastern Woodland tribes.

LAND AND SEA

Traditional Micmac life followed a pattern dictated by the seasonal availability of food. For much of the year—from spring until fall—the Micmac lived on the coast in villages lying between the sea and a river or stream. These sites provided them with the mainstay of their diet: fish, shellfish, and game animals, as well as the occasional seal and whale. In late summer the women gathered berries and dug up ground nuts. Some foods were dried for winter use.

As winter approached, the Micmac moved inland, once again establishing a campsite near a river or stream that provided an abundance of food, particularly fall runs of eels and migrating ducks and geese. In winter the Micmac tribespeople trapped moose, deer, beaver, bear, and caribou or hunted them with bows and arrows.

Throughout the year nuclear families (small families made up of a husband and wife and their children) lived in birchbark wigwams, while extended families (larger families made up of several generations of relatives) sheltered in larger, rectangular birchbark structures. In winter additional protection from the cold was provided by placing mats and animal skins over the birchbark. Sometimes a Micmac village was surrounded by a palisade—a fence of wooden stakes—to fortify it against enemy raids.

POLITICAL AND SOCIAL LIFE

The Micmac nation was divided into seven districts. Each district had a chief, under whom there were local chiefs in charge of specific territories. At the head of all these chiefs was the Grand Chief, or sagamore. The Micmac tribes came together to decide policies affecting the whole nation. These meetings were attended by

BELOW: Micmac craftwork was adapted to European demands. This Micmac chair seat is decorated with porcupine quills—a traditional Micmac craft.

local and district chiefs and by other men who were particularly respected in the community.

The Micmac were a warlike people whose enemies included the Mohawk and the Algonquian tribes of New England. They sometimes fought the Subarctic Inuit and Malecite too. Although they were aggressive, the Micmac adopted captured women and children into their own community.

Feasts were an important part of Micmac life and were held for a variety of major and lesser events, such as the marriage of a daughter, a funeral, or a child's first tooth.

Micmac men often took more than one wife. The women prepared and gathered food, and made clothing and household objects such as reed baskets and woven mats. The men hunted and fished.

THE MICMAC TODAY

The Micmac suffered greatly from the arrival of the Europeans. Disease, alcohol, genocide (murder of a race), and loss of traditional lands all resulted in a staggering decline in the Micmac population. The total number of Micmac people before the arrival of the Europeans is not known, but reports from early settlers, missionaries, and traders suggest they were a powerful and important tribe in the area. By 1850 the total Micmac population was a mere 3,000.

In 1867 the federal government of Canada finally took responsibility for the Micmac. But it was not until more than 100 years later that the Micmac and other tribespeople came together to establish effective

ABOVE: The Micmac used fine quillwork to decorate their artifacts, such as this small box.

political unions, such as the Union of Nova Scotia Indians and the Union of New Brunswick Indians, both formed in 1969.

Today the Micmac are pursuing land claims and damages from the federal government and have had some success in reclaiming hunting and fishing rights. The Micmac are becoming increasingly aware and proud of traditional practices such as powwows, or meetings, yet their lifestyle is a mix of the traditional and the modern.

SEE ALSO:

- Alcohol
- Algonquian
- Birchbark
- Bows and Arrows
- Disenfran- chisement
- Epidemics
- Fishing
- Fishing Rights
- Fur Trade
- Hunter- gatherers
- Inuit
- Land Rights
- Marriage
- Mohawk
- Quillwork and Beadwork
- Warriors
- Women
- Woodland

Midewiwin

The *Midewiwin*, or Great Medicine Society, is a major ceremony of the Algonquian tribes of the Great Lakes region. Although it is still performed today, it is highly secretive, and only people who have been instructed in its rituals are allowed to see it or to participate in the ceremony.

MANABOZHO'S LEGACY

The *Midewiwin* is said to have been given to the people by an ancient shaman (medicine man) called Manabozho, who founded the original lodge in which the ceremonies were held. He did this as a way of offering thanks to the Great Spirit, or Manitou, after the different supernatural beings helped him overcome his grief following the death of his brother.

The rituals of the *Midewiwin* are intended to benefit and bring good health to the whole tribal community. The rituals are conducted by shamans who are said to possess knowledge passed down to them by Manabozho. They in turn are able to pass this knowledge on to other members of the tribe who wish to help the community.

When Manabozho set up the first *Midewiwin* lodge, he used the otter spirit to show people how to live in relation to Manitou. Otters move quite easily between land and water. The Ojibway, among whom the *Midewiwin* was particularly important, saw this as representing the ease with which a shaman should be able to move between the spirit and the natural worlds. The otter then became the *Midewiwin*'s symbolic creature.

ABOVE: A bag made from the paw and claws of a bear marked the second level of *Midewiwin* membership.

THE STRUCTURE OF THE SOCIETY

Originally the *Midewiwin* was organized into four—or sometimes eight—layers of membership. The least prestigious layer had the most members; the most prestigious, the fewest. Greater prestige came with greater knowledge of the mysteries of Manitou but also reflected the wealth of the member. The reason that the wealthier members obtained greater prestige was that the duties a member had to perform became progressively more expensive.

The symbols of the *Midewiwin* were small white shells known as *migis*. These were thought to carry the power of the spirit world and were sewn into bags representing different levels of leadership. Each of these levels was associated with an animal spirit such as the bear, beaver, white martin, or weasel.

INITIATION CEREMONY

A person was initiated into the *Midewiwin* by means of a special ceremony that represented death of the human form followed by rebirth as a mixture of spirit and human. Shamans "shot" the *migis* into the person being initiated by throwing the bags at them. This made the person fall to the ground in a faint.

The *Midewiwin* shamans then placed the bags on the unconscious person. Soon after, the person would revive. From that moment onward that person possessed the power of the *Midewiwin.*

These initiations continue today, and are traditionally held once a year, normally in late spring or early fall. They last as long as it takes to initiate all the candidates.

SEE ALSO:

- Algonquian
- Birchbark
- Crow
- Iroquois
- Longhouse Religion
- Masks
- Medicine
- Medicine Bundle
- Ojibway (Chippewa)
- Plains
- Ritual
- Shamanism
- Tobacco

BELOW: Ojibway members of the *Midewiwin* drew seating plans for their meetings on strips of birchbark as a memory aid.

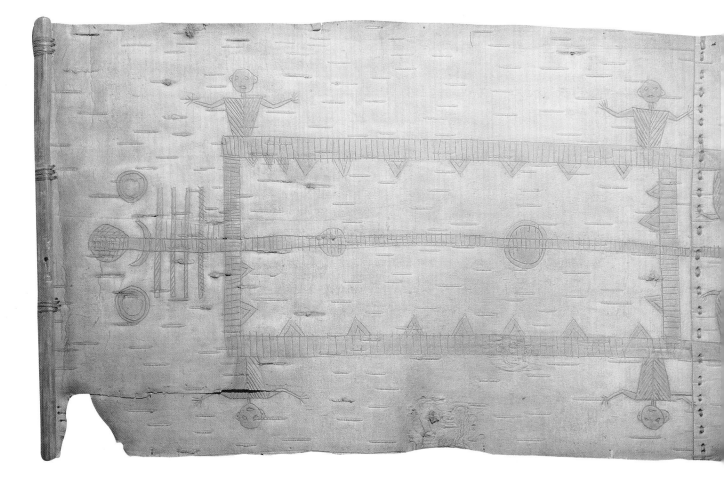

Mission Indians

Mission Indians were those Native Americans who, from about the 1650s to the middle of the 19th century, were forced to live in missions—settlements run by European Christian missionaries. There were mission Indians in various parts of North America, including Florida, Quebec, and the Northwest Coast. However, the term is most often applied specifically to the many Native American tribes in California who came under the control of Catholic missionaries from Spain in the 18th century.

This is because the missions founded in California by Spanish Franciscan and Dominican priests were among the largest and because they so fundamentally changed the lives of so many Native Americans, causing them to lose their tribal identities and cultures. The California missions were also among the most brutal in the whole of North America.

THE LEGACY OF COLUMBUS

After the arrival of Columbus in the Americas in 1492 the Spanish conquistadors, or conquerors, worked their way through the West Indies and Central and South America, cruelly subduing the native inhabitants and taking over their lands. By the middle of the 18th century they had begun to establish *presidios*, or forts, and *rancherias*, or ranches, in Baja California, which is now part of Mexico. They also began to set up the first church-run missions.

At that time there were many Native Americans living in California. These tribes had lived in the

BELOW: Diegueno mission Indians like these men and women were named after the mission at San Diego, but they came from different original tribes.

same way for hundreds of years in peaceful and settled local communities. Most of them lived in very small villages made up of only a few related families. This was because the environment of California was such that virtually all their needs could be provided for within a small area. Most tribes were hunter-gatherers, whose staple diet was acorns, which they ground

33

up into soup or bread-meal. They hunted rabbit, deer, and quail, fished for salmon, and gathered wild foods such as ryegrass seeds, camas roots, plums, grapes, and manzanita berries.

The Spanish, however, totally disregarded local custom when they arrived in California. To them, all Native Americans were heathens whose souls could be redeemed, or saved, only by converting them to the Christian faith. The most efficient way to do this was to gather the small tribes into large groups for instruction by priests.

The Spanish herded local people together in the missions regardless of their different tribal identities. Many of these people could not even understand each other, since they spoke different languages. Spanish missions undermined local tribes to such an extent that often we no longer know their original identities—the Fernandeno people, for example, were simply all those different people brought together in the mission at San Fernando.

FORCED INTO SLAVERY

The Spanish arrived in California in 1769, when a Franciscan missionary called Father Junipero Serra reached the area of what is now San Diego. When he met the Ipai and Tipai tribes there, he wrote: "Believe me, when I saw their general behavior, their pleasing ways and engaging manners, my heart was broken to think that they were still deprived of the light of the Holy Gospel." Serra enlisted the help of the Spanish army in rounding up the local tribes and forcing them to work for him on

BELOW: Watched by local Native Americans, Spanish Father Junipero Serra oversees the raising of the Cross on Presidio Hill on his arrival at San Diego Bay in California in 1769.

ABOVE: Women receive instruction in a mission in California.

his missions. In total he and other Franciscan priests established 21 missions along the California coast, from San Diego to San Francisco.

The declared aim of the missions was to enlighten the Native Americans through teaching them Christianity. In reality the tribes served as an army of forced labor for the Europeans. The missions were barracks rather than churches, where Native-American peoples were herded together to work as slaves on the land. If they tried to escape, they were whipped with barbed lashes or put into solitary confinement without water. Sometimes they were branded, tortured, or even executed. The Native-American recruits—or neophytes, as they were called—were given Spanish names, made to wear uniforms, and forced to worship as Catholics; their own spiritual beliefs were regarded as primitive. They were given poor shelter, sanitation, and food, and family members were separated. Many died from diseases such as smallpox or from the brutal punishments meted out to them.

TRIBES UNITE IN REVOLT

The Californian Native Americans were not aggressive people, but eventually they rebelled against their enslavement. In 1775 the Ipai and Tipai tribes united to burn down the mission at San Diego. The rebellion took the Spanish a year to put down. Ten years later a Native-American medicine woman, or shaman, named Toypurina led a failed attempt to destroy the San Gabriel mission east of Los Angeles.

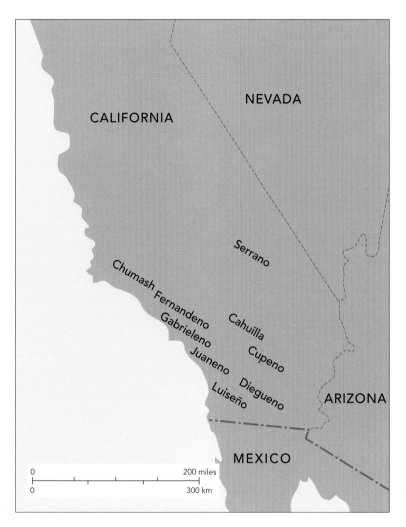

CALIFORNIA

NEVADA

Serrano

Chumash
Fernandeno
Gabrieleno
Juaneno
Cahuilla
Cupeno
Luiseño
Diegueno

ARIZONA

MEXICO

0   200 miles
0   300 km

mission Indians. Their villages were gone, and many of them starved when the missions closed or were turned into ranches. Those mission Indians who remained on the ranches continued to work as poor laborers. In 1848 the U.S. took control of California from the Mexicans, and the famous Californian gold rush started. This meant that former Native-American lands were now settled by white immigrants.

TOO LITTLE, TOO LATE

By the late 19th century the U.S. government finally began to establish reservation lands for the Native Americans, but by then it was too late. Most of the former Native-American homelands were now owned by whites. In addition the Native-American population had been decimated: where in 1769 there had been over 300,000 Native Americans in California, by 1900 there were only 10,000 left. In the 20th century their numbers began to increase, though, as the different Californian tribes struggled to reclaim their lost identities.

During the 18th century there were many revolts, most notably by the Chumash at La Purisma, Santa Ynez, and Santa Barbara missions. But despite their efforts to free themselves, many of the Chumash rebels were later rounded up and returned to their missions, while others were executed or sentenced to forced labor in chaingangs.

During the 19th century the Mexican government, which had won independence from Spain, ended the church's right to imprison Native-American people against their will. However, this created new problems for the

ABOVE: This map shows the original locations of the main Californian mission Indians. The original tribal identities of many mission Indians are no longer known. The name "Luiseño," for example, refers to all the different people who were gathered together in the mission at San Luis.

SEE ALSO:
❖ Californian
 Tribal Groups
❖ Chumash
❖ Disenfran-
 chisement
❖ Epidemics
❖ Extinction
❖ Fur Trade
❖ Iroquois
❖ Land Rights
❖ Legislation

❖ Missions
❖ Mohawk
❖ Pan-Indian
 Movement
❖ Population
 Density
❖ Poverty
❖ Recognition
❖ Reservations
❖ Shamanism
❖ Spain, Wars with

Missions

From about the 1650s onward European missionaries tried to convert Native Americans to Christianity and forced many of them to live in settlements called missions. The effect on tribal identities and cultures was profound.

Religion was always at least partly involved when Europeans and Native Americans met, whether as friends or enemies. European pastors and priests felt it was their Christian duty and responsibility to "educate" and "civilize" Native Americans, as well as convert them.

COUNTING THE CONVERTED

Spain was a leader in missionary activity. Its armies of conquistadors, or conquerors, were accompanied by Catholic priests who set up missions in Florida, the Southwest, and California. In Florida only Native Americans in missions were counted and recorded in population censuses, since Spanish law decreed that only converted Native Americans had souls. In California many small tribes lost their separate identities and cultures when they were forced to live together in groups in large Spanish missions.

Other European powers tried to convert Native Americans to their own particular Christian churches. French Jesuit missionaries, in competition with English Puritans, actively helped the French make trading links with Native Americans from their bases in Quebec.

The Catholic Jesuits and Protestant Puritans both established settlements of converted Native Americans. The Puritans founded Quinnipiac reservation in New

ABOVE: San Carlos de Borromeo, shown here in a painting from around 1830, was a Spanish mission in California (then part of Mexico).

Haven in 1638, while the Jesuits founded Caughnawaga Mohawk Reservation in Quebec in 1676.

On the Northwest Coast, among the Inuit, Aleut, and Tlingit peoples of British Columbia and southern Alaska, the Russian Orthodox Church was granted a royal monopoly (exclusive control) in 1799. From there it spread its influence south to the Pomo tribes of California. Russian religious activity, like that of the French, was linked with trade. This meant that Native Americans were converted not just to save their souls but also so they could be exploited as cheap labor.

RESISTANCE TO MISSIONS

In many cases there was Native-American resistance to missionary activities. The Tlingit, for instance, rose against the Russian garrisons when the Russians took power

LEFT: This woven basket bowl was made in the 19th century by Native Americans in a California mission.

away from their shamans (medicine men or women). They gave in only when a fleet of Russian warships armed with cannon attacked their villages.

In other cases there was little or no resistance. The Native Americans followed Christian rituals inside the mission churches but held traditional dances in the plazas outside. This practice is still common among the Pueblo tribes of the Southwest.

LASTING INFLUENCE

Many Pan-Indian movements were significantly influenced by Christianity. The Smohalla Cult, John Slocum's Indian Shaker Church, and Wovoka's Ghost Dance religion were all led by prophets who taught a combination of Christian and Native-American beliefs.

At the start of the 20th century the last great Native-American prophet, the Comanche leader Quanah Parker, helped found the most widespread Pan-Indian religion of today: the Native American Church. It uses peyote—a cactus that produces the drug mescal—for the sacrament and to induce hallucinations and visions. It combines this practice with Christian beliefs— taken from various sections of the Christian churches—that were taught by missionaries and promoted by them through the mission system. The Native American Church was legalized in 1934, and about half of all Native Americans living in the United States today are members.

The mission system started as a way of destroying Native-American beliefs and replacing them with various forms of European Christianity. In the process it destroyed tribal cultures and identities. Today the Native American Church is a unifying force in reestablishing awareness of both.

SEE ALSO:
- Californian Tribal Groups
- Ghost Dance
- Inuit
- Mission Indians
- Mohawk
- Pan-Indian Movement
- Parker, Quanah
- Peyote
- Pomo
- Pueblo
- Russia, Wars with
- Shamanism
- Tlingit
- Trade
- Wovoka

Mississippian

The Mississippians, or Temple Mound Builders, were expert farmers who lived on the rich floodplains of rivers in the Southeast. There they grew corn, beans, squash, pumpkins, and tobacco. After they imported improved varieties of corn from Mexico about A.D. 700, the Mississippians began to establish big ceremonial and trade centers with large populations. The largest of these, Cahokia, across the Mississippi River from present-day St. Louis, may have had a population as high as 30,000.

The most notable features of Mississippian sites are flat-topped earth mounds or pyramids. On top of these stood temples built of mud and thatch, which were looked after by a special caste of priests. These mounds, together with smaller mounds that supported housing for the nobles, usually formed an inner sanctum, or sacred place, which was protected by palisades (fences built of stakes).

Outside the town centers there were cultivated fields and a number of small communities that depended on the larger ones for their resources.

AN ORDERED SOCIETY

Mississippian culture was organized as a system of ranked hereditary positions with a male leader or chief, who also acted as the high priest. It was believed that he obtained his position through divine sanction. However, he inherited his power from his mother's side of the family, and it was essential that she was of noble birth. Below the chief or high priest was a class of aristocrats or nobles, and below them were various honored professionals. Most of the population were commoners—a kind of working class—and beneath them were slaves, who were often captives from enemy tribes.

Mississippian culture had two main divisions: one was associated with the Siouan-speaking people of the eastern Woodland, and the other was a western tradition associated with the Southern Cult. The Southern Cult was strongest in the Caddoan-speaking areas of modern-day Texas, but it spread across the South to Georgia and

BELOW: This pot of the Southern Cult is in the form of a severed head, with the mouth and eyes sewn shut.

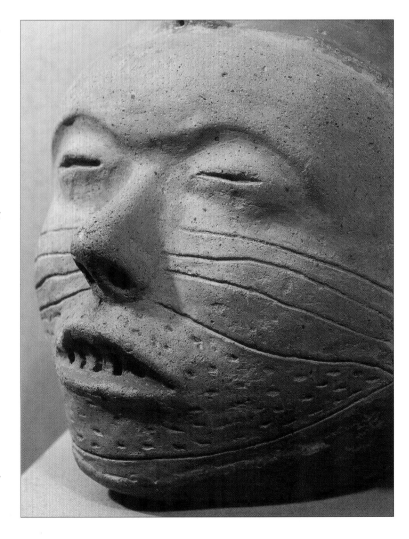

LEFT: Woodpeckers, symbols of war, encircle the sun on this shell gorget (throat armor) of the Southern Cult.

the decline of the Mississippian culture, including overpopulation, crop failure, and political strife.

The last surviving remnant of Mississippian culture was still being practiced by the Natchez tribe when they were contacted by Hernando de Soto, a Spanish conquistador, or conqueror, in 1542. It continued until the Natchez were defeated in the 1730s by French soldiers and Choctaw mercenaries. The remaining Natchez fled as refugees to live among their former enemies, the Chickasaw, Creek, and Cherokee peoples.

had some influence throughout the Mississippian area. Human sacrifice was a familiar theme in the arts of the cult, which performed ceremonies at major sites and became fully developed after A.D. 1000.

BELOW RIGHT: Crying eyes, as shown here on this pot, were one of the symbols used by the Southern Cult.

SOUTHERN CULT ARTIFACTS

Human sacrifice is depicted on sculpture, pottery, masks, copper sheets, and gorgets (throat armor) from Southern Cult sites. Pots often take the form of the severed heads of captives, with the eyes and lips sewn shut. Other images include hunchbacked female figures and pipes in the shape of animals and birds. Also depicted are stylized symbols—skulls, bones, elaborate crosses, and the form of a weeping eye—that seem to be specifically associated with the practices and beliefs of the Southern Cult.

Most of the major Mississippian sites were abandoned before the period of European contact. Many reasons have been suggested for

SEE ALSO:
❖ Adena and Hopewell
❖ Caddoan Speakers
❖ Cahokia
❖ Death Customs
❖ Mound City
❖ Mound Spiro
❖ Natchez
❖ Pottery
❖ Pyramids
❖ Serpent Mound
❖ Siouan Speakers
❖ Soto, Hernando de

Mitla

The remains of the Mixtec city-state of Mitla lie about 30 miles (48 km) east of the city of Oaxaca, in Oaxaca state in southern Mexico.

Unlike other Mixtec city-states, Mitla was built on the plains of a river valley, not on high ground. It was originally occupied by the Zapotec, who dominated the lands around the Valley of Oaxaca in the Classic period, which lasted from about A.D. 300 until about A.D. 900.

As the power of Monte Alban, the Zapotec center, declined in the seventh century, Mitla became a major satellite city. Mitla may have been inhabited by the Zapotec until the 10th century, after which there was a strong influence on the city-state from the Mixtec people.

LAND OF THE DEAD

The name "Mitla" comes from the Nahuatl (Aztec) word *mictlán*, meaning "land of the dead." Friar Burgoa, a Spanish missionary who visited the city in the 17th century, believed the name referred to the burial of Zapotec kings, nobles, and warriors in one of the five palaces, but no major burial sites have been found. He also reported that Mitla contained the residence of the high priest who presided over human sacrifices to the Zapotec gods.

The central part of Mitla covers about 0.8 square miles (2 sq. km). Outlying sites and agricultural areas total 8 square miles (20 sq. km). Many of the smaller outlying sites now lie in the center of the modern town of Mitla.

The main part of the city consists of four great palace complexes set around a series of plazas. Leading back into the complexes are various courtyards and patios connected by narrow passages.

The long, low palaces, similar to buildings found in the Mayan city of Uxmal in the Yucatán, suggest that trade and social contacts may have been established between the Mixtec and Maya civilizations.

MYRIAD MOSAICS

Mitla's most striking features are the beautiful Mixtec stone mosaics, often painted in white and red, that decorate the palace walls. The tiny stones were painstakingly set into panels one by one, without any mortar, to create more than a dozen different geometric patterns.

After the Spanish took over Mitla in the 18th century, they built a church on top of one of the city's palaces. Its present-day worshipers combine both Catholic and Zapotec traditions in their services.

ABOVE: The Hall of Columns was one of five palaces in the ancient Mixtec city-state of Mitla.

SEE ALSO:
- Afterlife
- Art
- Aztecs
- Death Customs
- Maya
- Missions
- Monte Alban
- Ritual
- Uxmal

Modoc

LEFT: The Modoc
traditionally made
baskets out of
woven tule bulrush.

When they first came into contact with white people, about the beginning of the 19th century, the Modoc lived along the Lost River and around the lakes along the borders of California and Oregon. They shared the area with the Klamath tribe—Klamath to the north, Modoc to the south—and spoke the same dialect of the Penutian language.

The Modoc way of life had more in common with the Plateau tribes to the East, such as the Paiute, Washoe, and Shoshoni, than with the Californian tribes. They were also unusual among Californian tribes in resisting white settlement.

There were no more than 2,000 Modoc in Pre-Contact times, and by the middle of the 19th century their numbers shrunk to a few hundred after a succession of epidemics.

MODOC VILLAGE LIFE
The Modoc lived in about 25 villages, each with its own head man and shaman (medicine man or woman) but came together as one community in a crisis. Everybody left their villages in spring and moved from camp to camp until fall, exploiting seasonal food supplies. In camp they lived in shelters made from frames of willow poles stuck into the ground, tied together at the top, and covered with mats woven from tule, a bulrush that grew abundantly in the lakes.

In winter, when snow could gather in 6-foot (2-m) drifts, the Modoc tribespeople returned to their villages. Here they lived in lodges, built in round pits 15–40 feet (4.5–12 m) wide and 3–4 feet (1–1.2 m) deep. Stout wooden poles around the edge supported a system of rafters. The Modoc covered the inside of this framework with woven grass mats and the outside with a layer of bark topped with earth from the pit. A hole in the middle of the roof served as a chimney for a fire directly below, a ventilator, a window, and an entrance and exit; the only way in or out of a lodge was by using a ladder. Usually, two or three families shared a lodge.

Each Modoc village also had a sweat house, a small, airtight lodge in which tribespeople poured water on heated rocks to produce steam. Men and women used it both for keeping themselves clean and for

religious rituals led by the shaman: mostly prayers to spirits of the moon, stars, sky, and animals.

FOLLOWING THE FOOD

Modoc men used nets, traps, hook and line, and spears to catch fish from the lakes and rivers. A seasonal favorite was salmon, caught as they swam upriver to spawn. The men made dugout cedar canoes or rafts of logs tied together with tule for fishing and hunted small game, deer, elk, and antelope.

Modoc women—who were responsible for virtually everything else—gathered wild plants and berries and dug roots, such as wild

RIGHT: Taken at the end of the Modoc War (1872–1873), this photograph shows Modoc men and women and their U.S. Army captors.

Fact File

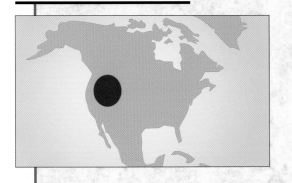

The Modoc lived on the Lost River and lakes of California and Oregon.

LANGUAGE:	*Penutian*
AREA:	*Basin and Plateau*
RESERVATION:	*Oklahoma, but most Modoc today live in Oregon*
POPULATION:	*2,000 Pre-Contact; approximately 600 today*
HOUSING:	*Shelters in summer, lodges in winter*
EUROPEAN CONTACT:	*Settlers in the 1840s*
NEIGHBORS:	*Klamath*
LIFESTYLE:	*Nomadic hunter-gatherers*
FOOD:	*Fish, game, and wild plants*
CRAFTS:	*Basketry*

potato. They used tule and other rushes and grasses to weave clothes and mats, and twined them together to create baskets.

In about 1800 the Modoc made indirect contact with white society. By trading with and raiding neighboring tribes, they acquired cloth and metal tools and pots for the first time. They also made contact with some Plains tribes. By the 1830s they were using horses and had begun wearing skins rather than woven clothing.

THE BEGINNING OF THE END
Late in 1843 a team lead by John Charles Fremont surveyed the Lost River area. As a result wagon trains began to come through Modoc territory in increasing numbers, following the Applegate Trail down into California. The increased traffic scared away much of the game in the area, and the Modoc began to go hungry. In 1847 an epidemic killed a third of the tribe. Modoc shamans decided the whites were

to blame for all the tribe's miseries. The Modoc attacked the next wagon train to come through, killing several dozen settlers.

GOLD RUSH LEADS TO WAR
An uneasy truce between the Modoc and the whites followed. Then, in 1851 gold was found nearby. Miners flocked to the area, displacing the Modoc. Skirmishes over land resulted in several deaths, mostly of Modoc who got in the way of a miner's claim. In 1852 a war party killed more than 70 whites at Tule Lake. In retaliation, Ben Wright of Yreka invited 46 Modoc leaders to peace talks and killed 41 of them. The bad feeling between the whites and the Modoc after these incidents came to a head in the Modoc War of 1872–1873, which ended with the tribe defeated and its leaders executed.

The survivors were sent to a reservation in Indian Territory, and some Modoc remain there today, in what is now Oklahoma.

SEE ALSO:
- Basin and Plateau
- Basketry
- Californian Tribal Groups
- Canoes
- Epidemics
- Fishing
- Homes
- Horses
- Hunter-gatherers
- Indian Territory
- Indian Wars
- Klamath
- Modoc War
- Paiute
- Plains
- Reservations
- Settlers
- Shamanism
- Sweat Lodge
- Wagon Trails

Modoc War

The Modoc people of what is now northern California and southern Oregon were involved in a number of violent clashes with white settlers from the 1850s onward. In 1864 the Modoc and the related Klamath people of southern Oregon made a treaty with the U.S. by which they gave up much of their land and agreed to move to a reservation in southern Oregon.

Unfortunately, the Modoc and Klamath tribes did not get on well together, and life on the reservation became intolerable for many Modoc people. Led by Kintpuash (called Captain Jack by white settlers), a band of Modoc left the reservation to return to their former home in

ABOVE: Kintpuash (nicknamed Captain Jack) was one of the last of the Modoc to surrender. His one-time ally Hooker Jim helped the U.S. soldiers find him. The night after he was hanged, graverobbers dug up his body. It was then embalmed and put on display in a traveling show.

the Lost River area near Tule Lake, where they lived for several years. In 1869 they were persuaded to return to the reservation, but they stayed only for a few months before leaving once again.

Late in 1872 the Bureau of Indian Affairs decided that Kintpuash and his followers must be forced to return to the reservation. In November soldiers arrived in Kintpuash's camp to do just that. A fight broke out, and one soldier and one Modoc were killed. Not long before this happened another Modoc band had had a series of clashes with white civilian vigilantes, killing 15 of them. This band, under a leader called Hooker Jim, united with Kintpuash and his people.

Together the Modoc took refuge in the area near Tule Lake, now called Lava Beds National Monument. They had a fighting force of only about 60 out of a total of some 170 people, but the barren, jagged, and twisted landscape of the lava beds provided excellent defensive positions.

THE BEGINNING OF THE WAR

In January 1873 the U.S. Army tried to expel the Modoc from what the whites now called Captain Jack's Stronghold. Over 300 soldiers, backed by an artillery barrage, moved toward Kintpuash and his men. About 40 of the soldiers were killed or wounded by Modoc snipers before the attack was called off. During the attack none of the soldiers even saw the enemy.

Kintpuash now realized it was time to negotiate and make the best deal he could. He told the army

LEFT: U.S. Army soldiers watch for Modoc snipers in the lava beds, while a reporter from the San Francisco *Bulletin* takes notes.

commander, General Edward Canby, that he and his people wanted only to be allowed to live among the lava beds, pointing out that these were valueless to the white settlers. General Canby could not agree to this, however, because it would have meant conceding victory to the Modoc, and the talks broke up at that point.

Another meeting was arranged for April 11, 1873. Kintpuash thought he could persuade General Canby to change his mind, but other Modoc warriors wanted Kintpuash to kill the general as a warning to the army to stay away.

Kintpuash predicted that killing General Canby would only make the army so angry that they would crush the Modoc completely. Most of his people disagreed, however, so he reluctantly decided to go along with their plan. When the meeting took place, Kintpuash duly shot dead General Canby.

Kintpuash was proved right, for the army now sent in over 1,000 men, including a number of Apache scouts, against the tiny force of Modoc. Despite massive attacks, backed by ferocious artillery fire, the Modoc were not immediately defeated. Instead, they picked off their white attackers almost at will. On one occasion in late April they ambushed a detachment of about 70 men, killing or wounding more than half of them.

DELAYING THE INEVITABLE

These successes only disguised the true position, however. The Modoc were fast running out of food and water and knew that they could not go on fighting forever. By the end of May 1873 many of them had surrendered. Kintpuash and his family were among the last to give up, at the start of June. He and three other leaders were subsequently tried and hanged for the murder of General Canby.

The few surviving Modoc were shipped to a reservation in the Indian Territory, but some of their descendants were allowed to return to the Klamath reservation in 1909.

SEE ALSO:
❖ Apache
❖ Bureau of
  Indian Affairs
❖ Indian Territory
❖ Klamath
❖ Modoc
❖ Reservations
❖ Treaties

Mogollon

The Mogollon, or Mountain People, are named after the small, twisting mountain range that runs along the border between southern Arizona and New Mexico, where they established settlements in the high valleys. They were the first prehistoric people of the Southwest to practice agriculture on a regular basis—starting about the third century A.D.—with crops of corn, beans, tobacco,

BELOW: A hole was broken through this 10th-century Mimbres burial bowl—which shows childbirth—to help release its spirit into the next world.

squash, and cotton. The Mogollon did not develop the more sophisticated farming techniques of their Anasazi and Hohokam contemporaries but relied on digging-sticks for preparing the soil and on mountain streams for irrigation.

As a result the Mogollon remained dependent on supplementing the limited amount of food that they were able to grow by hunting small birds and animals and by gathering roots, berries, seeds, nuts, and insects.

Their agricultural efforts did, however, lead to the establishment of permanent villages along ridges above the valleys where they grew crops. These were easier to defend than valley settlements. Their villages consisted of pit houses made from log frames covered with roofs of saplings, reeds, and mud. Later they also built a few larger buildings to serve as *kivas*—ceremonial and meeting houses.

SKILLED ARTISANS

Although much of their handicraft was relatively unsophisticated, the Mogollon were skillful weavers. Fragments of clothing and blankets made from cotton, feathers, and fur yarn have been found by archaeologists at Mogollon sites. The Mogollon were excellent basket makers, too, and also produced a variety of stone, wood, and bone artifacts.

After about A.D. 1000 the Mogollon came increasingly under the influence of the Anasazi. One

region. Many Mimbres pots are beautifully painted shallow bowls, with mythical people, animals, and birds depicted in black and white. These designs show a sense of pattern and movement unequaled in any other pottery of the period.

Almost all Mimbres pots recovered from excavations had been ritually "killed" by having a hole broken through the center—this released the pot's spirit into the next world. Most Mimbres pots have been found with burials, so they were probably made specifically as grave offerings. There is no indication they had any other function.

SUDDEN DEPARTURE

The Mogollon's unique culture declined rapidly after A.D. 1200 and had disappeared completely by A.D. 1400. Mysteriously, at some point the last of the Mogollon abruptly abandoned their villages—nobody knows why. Most of the survivors were absorbed into Anasazi communities. Only a few retained their separate, Mogollon identities: it is their blood that flows in the veins of the modern Zuni.

consequence of this, and of their growing population, was that the Mogollon abandoned their pit houses in favor of above-ground pueblos made from adobe—bricks of sun-dried clay mixed with straw.

ABOVE: Made in the 10th century, this Mimbres burial bowl is decorated with the guardian spirits of the points of the compass.

FABULOUS POTTERY

Following the example of the Anasazi, the Mogollon also improved on their crude pottery of brown, coiled clay by covering it with a fine slip before firing it. This allowed them to paint it with intricate geometric designs.

The most dramatic—and best-known—product of Mogollon culture comes from a small group who lived in southwestern New Mexico. These people, known as the Mimbres, produced some of the most exquisite and distinctive pottery of the prehistoric Southwest

SEE ALSO:

Mohawk

The Mohawk played an important role in the Iroquois League of Nations. As the most eastern of the tribes of the league they were known as the Guardians of the Eastern Door. They were responsible for preventing enemy attacks undermining the league's hold over the Mohawk Valley in New York. They were also known as the Receivers of Tribute.

The Mohawk were feared by most other tribes and derive their name from an Algonquian word, Mohowauuck, which means "they eat live things" or "man-eaters." They earned this reputation because although the Mohawk were the smallest tribe in the league, they were also the most aggressive.

This was evident in 1648 when the Mohawk, with Seneca allies, broke a truce with another powerful Iroquois tribe, the Huron. Inside a year the greatly outnumbered Mohawk and Seneca warriors defeated the Huron and forced them to seek protection as refugees among other tribes. But the Mohawk could also be generous and forgiving, and they invited many of the refugees to found their own villages in Mohawk territory under Mohawk protection.

ALLIES OF THE BRITISH

During the French and Indian War, as well as in the American Revolutionary War, European nations and colonials vied with each other for Mohawk support. Most Mohawk were consistently friendly to the British and hostile to the French and Americans. Their famous leader, Thayendanegea, or Joseph

Brant, was even made a commissioned officer in the British army during the late 18th century.

With British support the Mohawk established communities in Ontario, free of American influence. Joseph Brant, for example, built a house at British expense, founding the town of Brantford. By being friendly with neighboring communities and adopting refugees from other tribes, the Mohawk thrived in Ontario. Their present population there of about 10,000 is perhaps twice the size of the original tribe.

The Mohawk also continue to enjoy their reputation for fearlessness. Today, a high proportion of the iron- and construction workers on the skyscrapers of New York City are Mohawk.

ABOVE: Mohawk moccasins were made from smoked hide and then decorated with beads and porcupine quill.

SEE ALSO:
- ❖ American Revolutionary War
- ❖ Brant, Joseph
- ❖ French and Indian War
- ❖ Huron
- ❖ Iroquois
- ❖ Quillwork and Beadwork
- ❖ Settlers
- ❖ Urban Life
- ❖ Warriors

Mohegan

The Mohegan tribe is sometimes confused with another Native-American tribe called the Mahican. The confusion arose following the publication in 1826 of a popular novel, *The Last of the Mohicans*, written by James Fenimore Cooper.

It is not clear which of the two tribes, the Mahican or the Mohegan, the author actually meant by "Mohican," but in any case his book is a work of fiction. It tells the story of Natty Bumppo, a frontiersman, whose best friend is Chingachgook, a Native-American brave. Chingachgook is the last surviving member of his tribe, the "Mohican." Cooper's adventure story—which has twice been made into a movie—captures the spirit of the Native-American Northeast but is not historically accurate.

Historical records show that the Mohegan and the Mahican are two related groups of Algonquian people. The original homelands of the Mohegan were around Connecticut. The Mahican lived along the northern end of the Hudson Valley—mainly in the present-day state of New York but also in Vermont and Massachusetts. Many Algonquian bands and villages near the Hudson River were united in a political grouping called the Mahican Confederacy.

BREAKAWAY GROUP

The Mohegan were an offshoot of the Pequot, a powerful, warlike tribe whose name is Algonquian for "destroyers." During the 17th century the Pequot competed with other Algonquian tribes for control

LEFT: Floral patterns, such as the one shown here, were introduced to the Mohegan by Europeans. The Mohegan adopted the designs and used them in their own quillwork.

of southern New England, where lush forests and quiet bays made hunting and fishing easy.

By 1620, when the pilgrims landed at Plymouth Rock, the Pequot had gained control of the area under their chief, Sassacus. Sassacus lived in a village on the Thames River, and under him were 26 lower chiefs, each with his own village. One of these lower chiefs, Uncas, broke away from the Pequot and formed his own group of supporters. This group became known as the Mohegan.

TRADITIONAL WAY OF LIFE

At the beginning of the 17th century the Mohegan had a way of life similar to most of the other Algonquian tribespeople in the Northeast at that time. The Mohegan lived in rectangular houses, their staple diet was fish, and they traveled by birchbark canoes.

However, the long-established Mohegan way of life soon changed as white settlers began to move into the area. The white immigrants fought against the Native Americans in the Northeast in the Pequot War of 1636, defeating Sassacus. Uncas made alliances with the whites and managed to hold on to power longer than his neighbors, but finally the whites turned against him and his people too.

The victorious whites took away the Mohegan's land and sold many of the Mohegan into slavery, along with members of the Wampanoag, Pequot, and Narragansett tribes. Other Mohegan died from European diseases, such as smallpox, to which they had no immunity.

Today the Mohegan, together with the Pequot, live on two small reservations in Connecticut and New York. To try to regain their homelands, in the early 1980s, the Mohegan filed a land claim and lawsuit against the state of Connecticut. However, it was vetoed by President Reagan. Today the tribespeople are seeking funds to help improve their poor standard of living and maintain their culture.

ABOVE: Made from smoked hide and black cloth and decorated with quillwork, this pouch is typical of the handicraft of the Northeast, such as the Mohegan.

SEE ALSO:
- Algonquian
- Algonquian Speakers
- Birchbark
- Canoes
- Epidemics
- Fishing
- Homes
- Hunting
- Land Rights
- Literature
- Movies
- Pequot War
- Poverty
- Quillwork and Beadwork
- Recognition
- Reservations
- Settlers
- Woodland

Monte Alban

The ruins of the ancient city of Monte Alban are about 6 miles (10 km) southwest of the city of Oaxaca in southern Mexico. The city was built on a mountain some 1,300 feet (400 m) above the Valley of Oaxaca and was occupied for 15 centuries. The first inhabitants were the Olmec, who were driven from the coastal areas of Veracruz to the north and Tabasco to the south by flooding about 500 B.C.

ZAPOTEC DOMINATION

The Olmec civilization mysteriously disappeared at the start of the Classic period, which lasted from about A.D. 300 to A.D. 900. During this time the Zapotec dominated Monte Alban and extended it by leveling and paving the mountain. Between 25,000 and 40,000 people lived in the city, and because of the limited space, the Zapotec built to the edges of the terraces. Another 50,000 may have inhabited the outlying settlements that sprang up throughout the valley.

By A.D. 600 Monte Alban was an imposing city of temples, palaces, pyramids, and plazas that covered 15 square miles (39 sq. km). One of the most intriguing buildings is the Palace of the Dancers, containing some of the earliest writing in Mexico. It also has a series of large stone carvings of Olmec "dancers," some of which are shown dissected or wounded. These may represent tortured prisoners or voluntary sacrifices, or may have been teaching aids for shamans (medicine men).

Monte Alban was a major site for burials and contains about 170 underground chambers for the dead. The earliest tombs were often just pits covered by stone, but later ones are highly decorated chambers reached by stairways. The wealth and prestige of the city's nobility is reflected in the burial objects. The Mixtec, who reused existing chambers, filled them with fine jewelry. Their intricate gold-work and fine bone-engraving were dramatically displayed in Tomb 7. Found in 1932, it contained 500 pieces of gold, silver, pearl, jade, alabaster, and turquoise jewelry.

Monte Alban was abandoned by the time the Spanish arrived in 1521. The city's decline began after increasing numbers of inhabitants moved to the valley floor and was accelerated by Aztec invasions during the 15th century.

LEFT: Most of Monte Alban's surviving structures were completed between A.D. 350 and A.D. 600, when the Zapotec culture dominated the city.

Mound City

Mound City is a series of ancient burial mounds 4 miles (6 km) from Chillicothe in Ross County, Ohio. They are among the most remarkable prehistoric earthworks in America.

The mounds were built by the Hopewell people, whose influence extended from the Ohio and Illinois rivers into the Midwest and East from 200 B.C. until about A.D. 500. Southern Ohio was one of the most important centers for the Hopewell, who constructed a number of mounds in the area.

Mound City is surrounded by a 3-foot (1-m) high artificial embankment of earth. The embankment is almost square but has rounded corners. Such "geometrical" enclosures are found in a number of Hopewell sites in southern Ohio and neighboring regions, including Hopewell Mounds, Seip Mounds, and Newark Works. It is believed that the low walls served a social and ceremonial purpose rather than a defensive one.

MOUNDS INSIDE AND OUT

The low-lying wall of Mound City encloses an area of approximately 13 acres (5 ha). There are 23 burial mounds within the present-day Mound City Park, with a further two mounds and numerous pits

BELOW: Although built nearly 2,000 years ago as sacred burial grounds, Mound City was used as a camp for troops in World War I. The site is now protected as a national monument in Mound City Park.

RIGHT: This mica snake is one of many exquisite artifacts found in archaeological excavations at Mound City.

outside it. The mounds served both as graves and as monuments to the people buried inside them.

MYSTERIOUS ALTAR MOUNDS

The remains of altars built on top of many of the Hopewell burial mounds provide further evidence of the religious significance of the earthworks. Most of the altars at Mound City were low, dish-shaped structures that varied in size but were all made of burned clay.

Many of the altars were damaged by reckless early excavations but have since been reconstructed. All the mounds with altars were built from alternating bands of gravel and thinner layers of sand. The reason for them is unknown. They may have had a symbolic meaning or a practical purpose.

The first careful investigation of Mound City was made in 1845 by a team led by the archaeologist, editor, and diplomat Ephraim George Squier and Edwin Hamilton Davis, an archaeologist and physician. A second excavation of the site was made by a group of archaeologists with the Ohio Historical Society in 1920 and 1921.

PIONEERING PUBLICATION

Squier and Davis visited Mound City while investigating more than 100 ancient earthworks in southern Ohio. Their detailed observations and descriptions formed part of their 1847 report, *Ancient Monuments of the Mississippi Valley.* It was a significant document because it was the first publication by the newly founded Smithsonian Institution. Moreover, Davis's extensive collection of artifacts found during the excavations revealed for the first time the extraordinary artistic development of the Hopewell.

Mound Spiro

Located in a narrow valley on the Arkansas River in eastern Oklahoma, Mound Spiro was a major Mississippian settlement and burial site. At its peak, from A.D. 1200 to A.D. 1400, it was the capital of a large chiefdom controlled by religious leaders and centered around the Arkansas River.

The settlement was first permanently occupied between A.D. 600 and A.D. 700. It gradually expanded to cover an area totaling 100 acres (40 ha) and containing a circle of 11 artificial earth mounds.

The lower, pyramid-type mounds were communal burial sites, while the community's elite were buried in two larger mounds. Other, platform-type mounds were used as bases for public structures.

PRIME LOCATION FOR TRADE

Mound Spiro flourished under the rule of a religious elite whose political influence extended to the Great Plains, the Mississippi Valley, and across the Southeast. The settlement occupied a strategic position on a bend in the Arkansas River between the farming tribes to the east and hunting tribes to the west. Its rulers exploited this natural gateway by making it a major trading center. Archaeologists have found large quantities of copper, mica, lead, quartz, greenstone, and shell artifacts. Such exotic materials reveal that the settlement's trading links extended from the Appalachian Mountains to the Gulf Coast.

The artifacts found at Mound Spiro include elaborate ornaments, jewelry, and ceremonial objects. Various techniques, including engraving and embossing, were used to decorate them with scenes of animals, people, and mythical beings. Such ornate objects reflect the prestige of the settlement's ruling elite as they grew in economic and religious importance.

Although Mound Spiro was a major center, it was used mainly for ceremonial and political purposes, and its population was relatively small. The inhabitants mainly farmed and gathered wild plants.

Mound Spiro declined as people in outlying settlements began to leave the region, while others moved farther along the Grand and Arkansas rivers. The inhabitants of Mound Spiro began to leave for the surrounding uplands, although they continued to use the mounds for burials. By 1450 the ruling priests had disappeared, and mound building at the site had stopped.

BELOW: Mound Spiro in eastern Oklahoma is now a National Historic Landmark.

SEE ALSO:
❖ Adena and Hopewell
❖ Art
❖ Death Customs
❖ Jewelry
❖ Mississippian
❖ Mound City
❖ Serpent Mound

Movies

Since the first days of film in the 1890s Hollywood has made more Westerns than any other kind of movie. Even allowing for artistic license, almost all portray Native Americans inaccurately. This is because they were made by white people for a white audience and are set in a mythical past in which white heroes "won" the West.

In most Westerns the immense cultural differences between Native Americans simply do not exist—they all live in tepees, wear feather headdresses, ride horses, and carry bows and arrows. They are also usually portrayed as one of three stereotypes: the Indian savage, who stands in the way of white civilization; the noble Indian, whose admirable but primitive way of life is doomed; and the Indian maiden, who usually falls in love with a white man and then dies tragically.

ORIGINS OF THE STEREOTYPES

Hollywood did not invent these stereotypes. As early as 1800 books and plays about Native Americans were more popular with white Americans than any other form of entertainment. In 1808 theater audiences were enthralled by *The Indian Princess, or La Belle Sauvage*, the

BELOW: In the early days of film Native Americans were often portrayed as savages in feather headdresses.

story of brave Pocahontas—the original Indian maiden. By 1840 there were more than 50 plays about her. The noble Indian originated in James Fenimore Cooper's frontier novels, such as *The Last of the Mohicans* (1826). Sentimental portraits of Native Americans from the past helped whites of the time avoid the problem of their own relations with Native Americans. Later, in the 1870s Buffalo Bill Cody traveled with his hugely successful Wild West show, called *The Scouts of the Prairie*, in which Native Americans were portrayed largely as Indian savages.

NOVEL ENTERTAINMENT

Audiences for the first, short silent movies of the early 1900s were mostly young, poor whites. They wanted cheap, unsophisticated entertainment, so Native Americans were portrayed as they had been in books and plays. The Indian savage was by far the most common stereotype because of the novelty of seeing outdoor action on screen, but the Indian maiden was quite popular too. In *Kit Carson* (1903) Indian savages murder a band of white fur trappers, but a squaw helps the white hero, Kit, escape, and then is killed for her good deed.

Cinema was still experimental, though, in these early days, and not all of the many hundreds of early movies made about Native Americans portrayed them in such a stereotypical way. In *The Indian Land Grab* (1910), for example, a sophisticated white woman falls in love with a Native-American man who is demanding land rights in

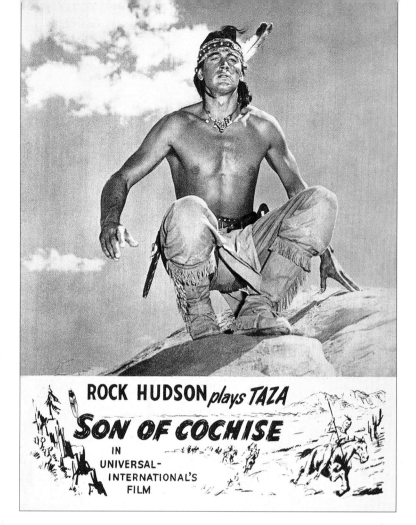

ROCK HUDSON *plays* TAZA
SON OF COCHISE
IN UNIVERSAL-INTERNATIONAL'S FILM

ABOVE: White stars have usually played leading Native-American roles in Westerns. In 1954 Rock Hudson was the star of *Taza, Son of Cochise*.

Washington D.C., helps him win them, and then goes to live with him and his people.

After 1912 longer, feature-length movies began to be made, with less experimentation. One exception was *The Silent Enemy* (1930), which attempts a realistic portrayal of the Ojibway's (Chippewa's) struggle to avoid starvation in the days before settlers—but it was a commercial failure. Generally, the emphasis was on action and daring stunts.

The 1930s and 1940s in particular were eras of low-budget, action-packed Westerns, mass produced by the big studios. Stars were signed to make several movies a year, and it was common to shoot two movies at once, and use the same action footage in both.

Not surprisingly, the Indian savage was the main stereotype in these movies—as it was in the big feature Westerns of the time. Epics such as *The Covered Wagon* (1934), *Stagecoach* (1939), and *Western Union* (1941) told of the triumph of white civilization over Indian savages and the wilderness. Many epics about Custer were made, all glorifying him as a white martyr: *They Died with Their Boots On* (1941), for example.

The Indian maiden was the least used stereotype in this era, while the noble Indian most commonly appeared as the white hero's loyal helper. Tonto, faithful companion of the masked Lone Ranger, features in several low-budget movies. But by and large the late 1940s saw the end of the low-budget Western.

Stereotypes persisted, but movie-makers became more aware of how white Americans have distorted the history of the West. In *Fort Apache* (1948) actor Henry Fonda plays an arrogant, racist fort commander whose refusal to negotiate with Cochise results in the massacre of his own troops. In *Broken Arrow* (1950) James Stewart stars as a man who studies Apache culture so that he can talk peace with Cochise. The Apache leader is portrayed as a man of honor and becomes the hero of the movie by refusing to break the negotiated treaty.

ERA OF THE DOOMED INDIAN

After *Broken Arrow* the noble Indian in the form of the doomed hero became the dominant stereotype. *Crazy Horse* (1953), *Sitting Bull* (1954), and *Geronimo* (1962) all treat their subjects sympathetically in this way. In some movies, such as *The Searchers* (1956), *Major Dundee* (1964), and *Ulzana's Raid* (1972), the Indian savage is used only to illustrate white savagery.

The early 1970s saw various attempts by white movie-makers to portray Native Americans authentically, but with limited success. *A Man Called Horse* (1970), for example, accurately portrays some aspects of Sioux culture, such as their homes, but misrepresents

LEFT: Chief Dan George starred in many Westerns, such as *Little Big Man* (1970) and *The Outlaw Josey Wales* (1976), in which he plays the stereotypical role of the doomed noble Indian.

others—notably the Sun Dance, which it shows as a barbaric test of bravery, not a sacred rite. After the mid-1970s traditional Westerns lost their box-office appeal, and few have been made since. In those that have, such as *Dances with Wolves* (1990), the Indian savage has vanished, but the noble Indian and the Indian maiden persist.

However, a few mainstream movies since 1975 have tried to deal authentically with Native-American life today. *Three Warriors* (1977), for example, deals sensitively with the struggles of young Native Americans to reconcile traditional and modern ways of life. On the whole, though, mainstream movie-makers have avoided authentic portrayals of Native-American life because such movies are usually commercial failures.

MORE SAY IN THE MATTER

In the early days of cinema Native-American actors were usually restricted to playing extras, with white stars playing Native-American speaking parts. Even in recent times

ABOVE: *Dances with Wolves* (1990) aimed for authenticity but still depicts Native Americans as noble Indian stereotypes.

SEE ALSO:
- Apache
- Cochise
- Crazy Horse
- Geronimo
- Land Rights
- Literature
- Little Bighorn
- Manifest Destiny
- Ojibway (Chippewa)
- Pocahontas
- Reservations
- Settlers
- Sioux
- Sun Dance
- Treaties
- Wagon Trails
- Women

Native-American roles have sometimes been given to non-Native Americans: in *Flap* (1970), for example, a comedy set on a reservation, the non-Native-American actor Anthony Quinn plays the leading Native-American role.

Since the late 1960s, though, Native Americans have become more involved in determining their on-screen roles. In 1966 Jay Silverheels founded the Indian Actors Workshop and the Indian Actors Guild to teach acting to Native Americans and promote their use in Native-American roles. In 1972 Kiowa author N. Scott Momaday's 1968 Pulitzer-Prize-winning novel *House Made of Dawn* was made into a movie, with a script written by him and with Native-American actors and financing.

The emergence of the American Indian Broadcasting Corporation means that Native Americans now take more part in the production of mainstream movies in which they figure. Native Americans therefore have much more say in how they are portrayed in movies nowadays.

Music

In many Native-American myths the Creator sang things into being and then provided the things with a natural song: the sighing of the wind, the mating cries of birds, the laughter of a bubbling brook, the steady rhythm of waves breaking on the shore. In traditional Native-American music, therefore, natural songs and rhythms predominate.

A Kwakiutl song from the North-west Coast, with its sharp and powerful rhythm, repeats the rhythmic pounding of the waves, while its melody echoes the cries of seagulls and the calls of ancestors. Similarly, when the Hopi Dawn-light-Youths and Butterfly-Maidens sang the Hevebe Tawi—songs for rain—their chanting and joyous clapping repeated the steady patter of rain sent by the Cloud God.

Songs form the basis of most Native-American music, but singing was usually accompanied by percussion instruments, such as drums, clappers, rasps, and rattles. These varied widely.

Tribes of the Northwest Coast used painted box-drums made from wood and suspended from ceiling beams, while Pueblo people of the Southwest used drums that were hollowed-out sections of large logs. The water drums of the Woodland Ojibway (Chippewa) and Iroquois had plugs to change the level of water inside and so alter their tone.

NATURAL MATERIALS

Other percussion instruments had similar characteristics but varied in detail. Northwest Coast rattles were made from wood, ones from the Plains from rawhide, and those used by Southeast and Southwest tribes from hollowed-out gourds. Iroquois rattles were made from the shells of small turtles and filled with pebbles or dried seeds, the exact

RIGHT: Dating from about 1900, this painting shows the Lenya, or flute, ceremony of the Hopi people.

LEFT: On the Plains and around the Great Lakes drums like this Comanche example were covered with rawhide, which could be loosened or tightened to change the pitch.

number of which often had ceremonial significance. Rasps were made from notched wood or the notched spine of a deer's shoulder blade—rubbing sticks along them produced the rasping sound.

WIND INSTRUMENTS

Some instruments had more specific uses. Small bone tubes with a hole near the center were used as bird calls by the Pueblo, while people of the Great Lakes used rolled birchbark trumpets to imitate bellowing moose. Long bird-bones were often used for double flutes and dance whistles. Cane flutes were unique to the Yuman tribes of southwestern California. End-flutes, which produced a haunting sound, were used by men of Plains and Great Lakes tribes for playing love songs on hillsides in the evening.

The Apache were unique in using a one-string fiddle, which they copied from Mexican violins. This has given rise to the present-day use of violins in *matachina* dances in the Southwest. These dances combine Native-American and Spanish elements, with the violins retuned to play Native-American rhythms and melodies.

Muskogean Speakers

Muskogean was one of the main languages spoken in North America in the 16th century. At that time probably 80,000 or more people spoke Muskogean dialects. They lived mostly in the Southeast area, from the Gulf of Mexico to Tennessee, from the Carolinas to Louisiana, and in parts of Florida.

The first Europeans to come to the area in the 1500s—the French and the Spanish—were more concerned with their own colonial interests and with converting tribes to Christianity than with studying local languages. The British also waged colonial wars in the area.

BELOW: This late 18th-century engraving depicts a Creek chief and his young son.

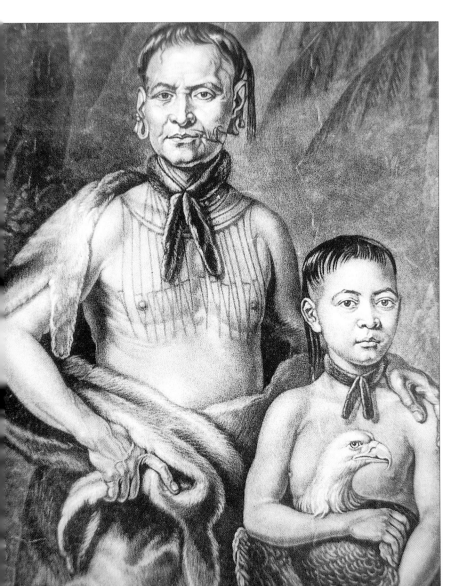

For these reasons we know only a little about the dialects of some of the smaller groups there.

Among the larger Muskogean-speaking tribes was the Chickasaw, whose regional dialect is so close to that of the Choctaw that the two tribes may originally have been a single group. They had already separated when the Europeans came, and the Chickasaw decided to support British interests, while the Choctaw became friendly with the French.

At this time the Choctaw population had increased to about 15,000, nearly twice the population of the Chickasaw. The Chickasaw, however, continued to enjoy a reputation for having the bravest warriors and opposed Choctaw and French plans for expansion. In fact, the Chickasaw warriors were so skilled that they not only resisted French plans but had also defeated large war parties from the Iroquois and from the Natchez tribes.

FLATTENED FOREHEADS

The Choctaw called themselves Chata, from the Spanish word *chato*, meaning "flattened" and referring to the peculiar flattened foreheads of the men. These were the result of strapping male babies into padded cradleboards while the bones of their skulls were still soft. The Choctaw considered them to be a mark of beauty.

The Chickasaw and Choctaw lived mostly in the areas of the modern-day states of Mississippi and Alabama: the Chickasaw in the north, and the Choctaw in the south, with some more villages in

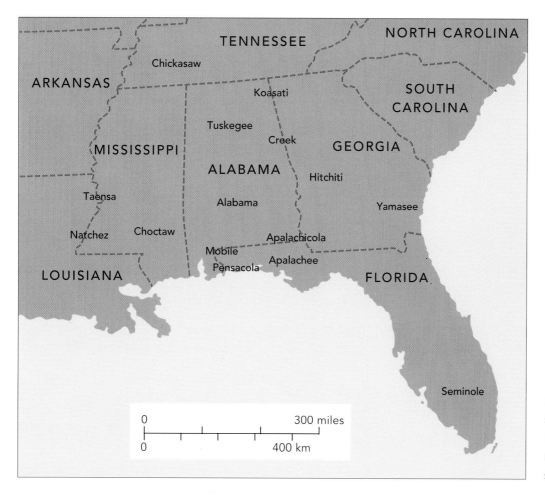

Georgia. Close by was another powerful Muskogean-speaking group, the Creek.

THE CREEK CONFEDERACY

The Creek population in the 1500s was about 30,000, twice that of the Choctaw. Unlike the Choctaw, they were not a single tribe but a confederacy of smaller groups who had banded together for mutual protection. The British called them the "Indians who live on the creeks," but other tribes knew them as the Muskogee, the "people of the swampy ground." Strangely, the word "muskogee," from which the term "Muskogean" derives, comes from the Algonquian language.

The Creek did not have a single term for the confederacy. Sometimes they called themselves Ochesee, meaning "true Creek," but most of the time each tribe within the confederacy used its own name.

The most important Creek tribe was the Hitchiti, whose dialect was adopted as the "official" Creek language. But there were many other dialects spoken in the confederacy, which even included tribes that spoke different languages.

Because of the size of the confederacy and the fact it was made up of many different tribes, the area it occupied was vast. It included North and South Carolina, Georgia, Alabama, and

LEFT: The Choctaw traditionally lived in rectangular houses made from wooden frames thatched with palmetto, or palm leaves.

parts of Florida. The Creek were always friendly to the British and hostile to the Spanish and French.

British expansion in the Southeast was, in fact, possible only because of Creek support. British–Creek armies destroyed the Spanish missions, drove out the French, and brought many smaller tribes under their rule. Important positions in Creek society were often held by people who were more British than Creek. For instance, the father of Creek chief Alexander McGillivray was a Scottish trader, while his mother was half-French, half-Creek.

The American Revolutionary War had a major effect on the Creek. Part of the confederacy supported the British; others, the Americans. Divisions in the confederacy gave rise to a new tribe of Muskogean speakers, the Seminole—from the Muskogean word *simanole*, meaning "separatists"—who established themselves in Florida.

OTHER MUSKOGEAN SPEAKERS

As well as the Chickasaw, Choctaw, Creek, and Seminole who, together with the Iroquoian-speaking Cherokee, later became the so-called Five Civilized Tribes of Oklahoma, a number of other groups in the area probably spoke dialects of Muskogean.

These other Muskogean speakers included the Natchez and Taensa of the Mississippi Valley, the Alabama, the Koasati, and Florida tribes such as the Calusa, Ais, and Guacata. Many of these small tribes either became extinct under the Spanish and the French or became refugees among larger tribes as a result of British–Creek activities.

SEE ALSO:
- Algonquian Speakers
- American Revolutionary War
- Birth Customs
- Children
- Extinction
- Five Civilized Tribes
- Homes
- Iroquois
- Missions
- Natchez
- Seminole
- Southeast/ Florida
- Warriors

A–Z of Native-American Tribes

This A–Z provides a cultural summary of the major Native-American tribes. Where a tribe is the subject of an article in a particular volume of this set, the volume number and page reference are given. Also, alternative historical names for some tribes are shown inside parentheses.

A

ABNAKI (Abenaki)
LANGUAGE: Algonquian
AREA: Northeastern Woodland
HOUSING: Conical bark or mat houses in palisaded villages
NEIGHBORS: Passamaquoddy, Penobscot, Malecite, Micmac
LIFESTYLE: Hunting, fishing, farming
FOOD: Deer, corn, fish
CRAFTS: Quillwork, birchbark, skinwork

ACOMA 1:4
LANGUAGE: Keresan
AREA: Southwest
HOUSING: Multistory adobe
NEIGHBORS: Pueblo, Apache, Navajo, Zuni
LIFESTYLE: Settled farmers
FOOD: Corn, gathered foods, game
CRAFTS: Pottery, weaving

ALEUT (Unangan)
LANGUAGE: Eskimo-Aleut
AREA: Arctic (Aleutian Islands)
HOUSING: Semisubterranean sod- and driftwood-covered shelters
NEIGHBORS: Inuit, Tlingit
LIFESTYLE: Sea-mammal hunting, fishing
FOOD: Seals, shellfish, fish, whales, seabirds, plant foods
CRAFTS: Basketry, ivory carving, gut clothing

APACHE 1:36
LANGUAGE: Athapascan
AREA: Southwest
HOUSING: Brush-covered wickiups, some use of tepees
NEIGHBORS: Pueblo, Navajo, Comanche, Kiowa, Paiute
LIFESTYLE: Nomadic hunting-gathering, some farming
FOOD: Game, roots, berries, some buffalo, some corn
CRAFTS: Basketry, skinwork

ARAPAHO 1:41
LANGUAGE: Algonquian
AREA: Central Plains
HOUSING: Tepees
NEIGHBORS: Cheyenne, Shoshoni, Ute, Kiowa, Pawnee, Sioux
LIFESTYLE: Nomadic hunting
FOOD: Buffalo, deer, roots and berries
CRAFTS: Skin-, bead-, and featherwork

ARIKARA (Ree, Sahnish)
LANGUAGE: Caddoan
AREA: Upper Missouri (Northern Plains)
HOUSING: Earth lodges
NEIGHBORS: Mandan, Hidatsa, Sioux, Pawnee
LIFESTYLE: Some farming, hunting
FOOD: Corn, buffalo, deer, gathered roots and berries
CRAFTS: Skinwork, featherwork

ASSINIBOINE 1:49
LANGUAGE: Siouan
AREA: Northern Plains
HOUSING: Tepees
NEIGHBORS: Blackfoot, Crow, Sioux, Cree
LIFESTYLE: Nomadic hunting
FOOD: Buffalo, deer
CRAFTS: Quill-, bead-, and skinwork

ATHAPASCAN, Northern (Dine or Dene) 1:54
LANGUAGE: Athapascan
AREA: Western Subarctic
HOUSING: Bark-covered wigwams, bark lean-tos, log houses
NEIGHBORS: Inuit, Tlingit, Cree, Blackfoot
LIFESTYLE: Nomadic hunting, fishing, gathering
FOOD: Caribou, wild fowl, fish
CRAFTS: Quillwork, birchbark

B

BELLA BELLA (Heiltsuk)
LANGUAGE: Wakashan
AREA: Northwest Coast
HOUSING: Split cedar plank
NEIGHBORS: Bella Coola, Kwakiutl, Haida, Tsimshian
LIFESTYLE: Sea-mammal hunting, fishing
FOOD: Sea mammals, salmon, shellfish, roots and berries
CRAFTS: Woodcarving

BELLA COOLA (Tallion)
LANGUAGE: Salishan
AREA: Northwest Coast
HOUSING: Split cedar plank
NEIGHBORS: Bella Bella, Kwakiutl, Coast Salish
LIFESTYLE: Sea-mammal hunting, fishing
FOOD: Sea mammals, salmon, shellfish, roots and berries
CRAFTS: Woodcarving

BEOTHUK 2:5
LANGUAGE: Beothukan
AREA: Eastern Subarctic
HOUSING: Birchbark lodges
NEIGHBORS: Inuit, Naskapi, Micmac
LIFESTYLE: Hunting-gathering, fishing
FOOD: Deer, salmon, shellfish, gathered roots and berries
CRAFTS: Woodwork

BLACKFOOT (Siksika, Kainah, Piegan) 2:14
LANGUAGE: Algonquian
AREA: Northern Plains
HOUSING: Tepees
NEIGHBORS: Shoshoni, Crow, Sioux
LIFESTYLE: Nomadic hunting
FOOD: Buffalo, deer
CRAFTS: Quill-, bead-, and skinwork

C

CADDO Confederacy (Kadohadacho) 2:38
LANGUAGE: Caddoan
AREA: Southern Plains
HOUSING: Domed thatched houses
NEIGHBORS: Choctaw, Chickasaw, Wichita
LIFESTYLE: Farming and hunting
FOOD: Buffalo, deer, corn
CRAFTS: Woodcarving, basketry

CALUSA
LANGUAGE: Muskogean
AREA: Southern Florida
HOUSING: Palm-thatched shelters
NEIGHBORS: Timucua
LIFESTYLE: Fishing, hunting
FOOD: Fish, shellfish
CRAFTS: Woodcarving

CAYUSE
LANGUAGE: Penutian
AREA: Plateau
HOUSING: Rush mat-covered lodges, some use of tepees
NEIGHBORS: Shoshoni, Nez Percé, Flathead
LIFESTYLE: Hunting, fishing
FOOD: Deer, salmon, roots and berries
CRAFTS: Basketry, skinwork

CHEROKEE (Tsaragi)
LANGUAGE: Iroquoian
AREA: Southeast
HOUSING: Palisaded townships of log cabins
NEIGHBORS: Creek, Catawba
LIFESTYLE: Farming, some hunting
FOOD: Corn, beans, squash
CRAFTS: Woodcarving, basketry

CHEYENNE 2:56
LANGUAGE: Algonquian
AREA: Central Plains
HOUSING: Tepees
NEIGHBORS: Shoshoni, Arapaho, Sioux
LIFESTYLE: Nomadic hunting
FOOD: Buffalo, deer, gathered roots and berries
CRAFTS: Skin-, bead-, and featherwork

CHICKASAW
LANGUAGE: Muskogean
AREA: Southeast
HOUSING: Palisaded townships
NEIGHBORS: Choctaw, Caddo, Natchez, Creek
LIFESTYLE: Farming, some hunting
FOOD: Corn, beans, squash
CRAFTS: Basketry

CHINOOK (Tsi-Nuk) 3:4
LANGUAGE: Chinookan
AREA: Southern Northwest Coast
HOUSING: Semisubterranean split-plank houses
NEIGHBORS: Coast Salish, Klikitat
LIFESTYLE: Trading, fishing
FOOD: Salmon, game animals, gathered roots and berries
CRAFTS: Woodcarving

CHOCTAW (Chata)
LANGUAGE: Muskogean
AREA: Southeast
HOUSING: Palisaded townships
NEIGHBORS: Natchez, Chickasaw, Creek
LIFESTYLE: Farming, fishing, hunting
FOOD: Corn, beans, deer, birds, turtles, fish, nuts and berries
CRAFTS: Split-cane basketry

CHUGACH
LANGUAGE: Inuit
AREA: Western Arctic
HOUSING: Sod- and driftwood-covered lodges
NEIGHBORS: Tlingit, Northern Athapascan
LIFESTYLE: Sea-mammal hunting, hunting, fishing
FOOD: Sea mammals, shellfish, fish, caribou
CRAFTS: Ivory carving

CHUMASH 3:7
LANGUAGE: Chumashan (Hokan)
AREA: California
HOUSING: Thatched huts
NEIGHBORS: Mission Tribes, Yokut
LIFESTYLE: Sea-mammal hunting, fishing, gathering
FOOD: Sea mammals, shellfish, fish, plants and berries
CRAFTS: Shellwork, stonework, basketry

COAST SALISH 3:15
LANGUAGE: Salishan
AREA: Southern Northwest Coast
HOUSING: Split-plank houses
NEIGHBORS: Kwakiutl, Chinook
LIFESTYLE: Fishing, sea-mammal hunting
FOOD: Salmon, shellfish, seal, sea birds, roots and berries
CRAFTS: Woodcarving

COMANCHE 3:20
LANGUAGE: Uto-Aztecan
AREA: Southern Plains
HOUSING: Tepees
NEIGHBORS: Kiowa, Apache
LIFESTYLE: Nomadic hunting
FOOD: Buffalo, other game, gathered roots and berries
CRAFTS: Skinwork, beadwork

CREE (Knistenaux) 3:38
LANGUAGE: Algonquian
AREA: Subarctic
HOUSING: Bark-covered wigwams
NEIGHBORS: Athapascan, Inuit, Blackfoot, Ojibway
LIFESTYLE: Nomadic hunting-gathering, trapping, fishing
FOOD: Game animals, fish, gathered roots and berries
CRAFTS: Birchbark, quillwork, beadwork

CREEK (Muskogee)
LANGUAGE: Muskogean
AREA: Southeast
HOUSING: Palisaded townships
NEIGHBORS: Choctaw, Chickasaw, Cherokee, Timucua
LIFESTYLE: Farming
FOOD: Corn, beans, squash, game
CRAFTS: Cane basketry, silverwork

CROW (Apsaroke) 3:42
LANGUAGE: Siouan
AREA: Northern Plains
HOUSING: Tepees
NEIGHBORS: Blackfoot, Assiniboine, Sioux
LIFESTYLE: Nomadic hunting
FOOD: Buffalo, deer, gathered roots and berries
CRAFTS: Skin-, bead-, and featherwork

D

DELAWARE (Leni Lenape) 3:56
LANGUAGE: Algonquian
AREA: Eastern Woodland
HOUSING: Palisaded villages of bark lodges
NEIGHBORS: Iroquois, Woodland Algonquian
LIFESTYLE: Farming, hunting
FOOD: Corn, game, fish, gathered plants and berries
CRAFTS: Woodcarving, beadwork

F

FLATHEAD
LANGUAGE: Salishan
AREA: Plateau
HOUSING: Semisubterranean earth- or brush-covered pit houses
NEIGHBORS: Cayuse, Coeur D'Alene, Nez Percé
LIFESTYLE: Fishing, gathering, hunting
FOOD: Salmon, buffalo, deer, roots and berries
CRAFTS: Basketry, beadwork

G

GROS VENTRE (Atsina)
LANGUAGE: Algonquian
AREA: Northern Plains
HOUSING: Tepees
NEIGHBORS: Blackfoot, Crow, Assiniboine, Sioux
LIFESTYLE: Nomadic hunting
FOOD: Buffalo, deer, gathered roots and berries
CRAFTS: Beadwork, skinwork

H

HAIDA 4:43
LANGUAGE: Haida (distant link to Athapascan)
AREA: Northwest Coast
HOUSING: Split cedar plank
NEIGHBORS: Tlingit, Tsimshian
LIFESTYLE: Sea-mammal hunting, fishing
FOOD: Salmon, sea mammals, seabirds, some plant foods
CRAFTS: Woodcarving, basketry, argillite (a type of rock) carving

HIDATSA (Minnetaree)
LANGUAGE: Siouan
AREA: Northern Plains
HOUSING: Earth-lodge villages
NEIGHBORS: Mandan, Arikara, Sioux
LIFESTYLE: Farming, seasonal buffalo hunting
FOOD: Corn, beans, squash, vegetables, buffalo
CRAFTS: Skinwork, beadwork

HITCHITI
LANGUAGE: Muskogean
AREA: Southeast
HOUSING: Palisaded villages
NEIGHBORS: Creek, Cherokee
LIFESTYLE: Farming, some hunting
FOOD: Corn, beans, squash, game
CRAFTS: Basketry

HOPI (Moki) 4:50
LANGUAGE: Uto-Aztecan
AREA: Southwest
HOUSING: Multistory adobe
NEIGHBORS: Pueblo tribes, Navajo, Apache
LIFESTYLE: Farming
FOOD: Corn, beans, squash
CRAFTS: Weaving, basketry, woodwork

HUPA 4:61
LANGUAGE: Athapascan
AREA: Northern California
HOUSING: Cedar plank houses
NEIGHBORS: Yurok, Karok, Pomo
LIFESTYLE: Fishing, hunting, gathering
FOOD: Salmon, shellfish, acorns, game, roots and berries
CRAFTS: Shell engraving, fiber weaving, basketry, featherwork

HURON (Wendat, Wyandot, Tobacco) 4:62
LANGUAGE: Iroquoian
AREA: Northeast Woodland
HOUSING: Palisaded villages of bark-covered longhouses
NEIGHBORS: Ojibway, Potawatomi, Iroquois
LIFESTYLE: Farming, some hunting
FOOD: Corn, beans, squash, deer, gathered plant foods
CRAFTS: Quillwork, splint basketry, fiber weaving

I

INGALIK
LANGUAGE: Athapascan
AREA: Arctic
HOUSING: Brush, bark, and driftwood shelters
NEIGHBORS: Inuit, Tlingit
LIFESTYLE: Fishing, hunting
FOOD: Salmon, caribou, moose, waterfowl, roots and berries
CRAFTS: Skinwork, woodcarving, basketry

INUIT (Eskimo) 5:14
LANGUAGE: Inuit
AREA: Arctic
HOUSING: Snow houses (igloos), whalebone and driftwood shelters
NEIGHBORS: Northern Athapascan, Tlingit, Cree
LIFESTYLE: Nomadic hunting and fishing
FOOD: Sea mammals, whales, fish, caribou, some gathered foods
CRAFTS: Ivory carving

IOWA
LANGUAGE: Siouan
AREA: Eastern Plains
HOUSING: Dome-shaped earth lodges, tepees when hunting
NEIGHBORS: Sioux, Omaha, Oto
LIFESTYLE: Farming, seasonal buffalo hunting
FOOD: Corn, buffalo, deer, some gathered foods
CRAFTS: Skinwork, beadwork, some carved stonework

IROQUOIS Confederacy (Five Nations, Six Nations) 5:20
LANGUAGE: Iroquoian
AREA: Northeast Woodland
HOUSING: Stockaded villages of elm-bark-covered longhouses
NEIGHBORS: Huron, Ojibway, Northeast Woodland Algonquian
LIFESTYLE: Farming, some hunting and fishing
FOOD: Corn, beans, squash, maple syrup, nuts, roots, deer
CRAFTS: Skinwork, splint baskets, woodwork, shellwork

K

KANSA (Kaw)
LANGUAGE: Siouan
AREA: Eastern Plains
HOUSING: Dome-shaped earth lodges, tepees when hunting
NEIGHBORS: Pawnee, Oto, Osage
LIFESTYLE: Farming, seasonal buffalo hunting
FOOD: Corn, beans, buffalo, deer
CRAFTS: Skinwork, beadwork

KAROK
LANGUAGE: Karok (Hokan)
AREA: Northern California
HOUSING: Plank houses
NEIGHBORS: Yurok, Modoc, Hupa
LIFESTYLE: Fishing, hunting, gathering
FOOD: Salmon, other fish, acorns, gathered roots and berries
CRAFTS: Basketry, shellwork, featherwork

KICKAPOO (Kiwigapaw)
LANGUAGE: Algonquian
AREA: Great Lakes
HOUSING: Bark lodges in semi-permanent villages
NEIGHBORS: Sauk and Fox, Potawatomi, Winnebago
LIFESTYLE: Hunting, farming, gathering
FOOD: Game, fish, corn, wild rice
CRAFTS: Barkwork, beadwork, woven bags

KIOWA 5:37
LANGUAGE: Tanoan
AREA: Southern Plains
HOUSING: Tepees
NEIGHBORS: Comanche, Wichita, Kansa
LIFESTYLE: Nomadic buffalo hunting
FOOD: Buffalo, deer, gathered roots and berries
CRAFTS: Skin-, bead-, and featherwork

KIOWA-APACHE
LANGUAGE: Athapascan
AREA: Southern Plains
HOUSING: Tepees
NEIGHBORS: Kiowa, Comanche
LIFESTYLE: Nomadic buffalo hunting
FOOD: Buffalo, deer, gathered roots and berries
CRAFTS: Skin-, bead-, and featherwork

KLAMATH 5:42
LANGUAGE: Klamath
AREA: Northern California
HOUSING: Plank houses
NEIGHBORS: Takelma, Yurok, Karok
LIFESTYLE: Fishing, hunting
FOOD: Salmon, acorns, game, gathered roots and berries
CRAFTS: Basketry, some shell- and woodwork

KUTCHIN (Loucheux)
LANGUAGE: Athapascan
AREA: Western Subarctic
HOUSING: Skin wigwams, log houses
NEIGHBORS: Northern Athapascan, Inuit
LIFESTYLE: Hunting, fishing, gathering
FOOD: Caribou, moose, salmon, herring, roots and berries
CRAFTS: Skinwork, beadwork

KUTENAI
LANGUAGE: Kutenai
AREA: Plateau
HOUSING: Bark- and mat-covered
NEIGHBORS: Pend D'Oreille, Nez Percé
LIFESTYLE: Hunting, fishing, gathering
FOOD: Buffalo, deer, fish, gathered roots and berries
CRAFTS: Basketry, beadwork

KWAKIUTL 5:44
LANGUAGE: Wakashan
AREA: Northwest Coast
HOUSING: Split cedar plank
NEIGHBORS: Nootka, Coast Salish
LIFESTYLE: Sea-mammal hunting, fishing
FOOD: Salmon, sea mammals, shellfish, roots and berries
CRAFTS: Woodcarving, basketry

M

MAIDU
LANGUAGE: Maidu (Penutian)
AREA: Northern California
HOUSING: Earth-covered lodges
NEIGHBORS: Pomo, Miwok
LIFESTYLE: Fishing, gathering
FOOD: Fish, acorns, game, gathered roots and berries
CRAFTS: Basketry, featherwork

MANDAN (Mihwatoni)
LANGUAGE: Siouan
AREA: Northern Plains
HOUSING: Stockaded villages of domed earth lodges
NEIGHBORS: Hidatsa, Arikara, Sioux
LIFESTYLE: Farming, seasonal buffalo hunting
FOOD: Corn, beans, buffalo, deer, roots and berries
CRAFTS: Skinwork, beadwork

MENOMINEE
LANGUAGE: Algonquian
AREA: Great Lakes
HOUSING: Semipermanent bark lodge villages
NEIGHBORS: Winnebago, Sauk and Fox
LIFESTYLE: Hunting, farming, fishing
FOOD: Corn, wild rice, game, roots and berries
CRAFTS: Woodwork, woven bags, quillwork

MICMAC 6:29
LANGUAGE: Algonquian
AREA: Northeast Woodland
HOUSING: Bark and grass mat- covered wigwams
NEIGHBORS: Beothuk, Northeast Woodland Algonquian
LIFESTYLE: Hunting, fishing
FOOD: Fish, shellfish, moose, caribou, waterfowl, plant foods
CRAFTS: Quillwork, birchbark

MISSION INDIANS 6:33
LANGUAGE: Mainly Uto-Aztecan and Hokan
AREA: Southern California
HOUSING: Thatch shelters
NEIGHBORS: Chumash, Mohave, Yuma
LIFESTYLE: Fishing, gathering
FOOD: Fish, shellfish, acorns, rodents, roots and berries
CRAFTS: Basketry

MODOC 6:42
LANGUAGE: Penutian
AREA: Northern California
HOUSING: Plank houses
NEIGHBORS: Yurok, Karok, Hupa
LIFESTYLE: Fishing, hunting, gathering
FOOD: Fish, shellfish, deer, gathered plants and berries
CRAFTS: Beadwork, basketry

MOHAVE (Mojave)
LANGUAGE: Hokan
AREA: Southwest
HOUSING: Domed thatch houses, sometimes covered with sand
NEIGHBORS: Yuma, Apache, Pima, Papago
LIFESTYLE: Hunting, fishing, gathering
FOOD: Deer, fish, gathered roots and berries
CRAFTS: Beadwork, pottery dolls, bark weaving

MOHEGAN 6:50
LANGUAGE: Algonquian
AREA: Eastern Woodland
HOUSING: Villages of bark-covered houses
NEIGHBORS: Iroquois, Northeast Woodland Algonquian
LIFESTYLE: Farming, hunting
FOOD: Corn, beans, deer, gathered roots and berries
CRAFTS: Basketry

MONTAGNAIS
LANGUAGE: Algonquian
AREA: Eastern Subarctic
HOUSING: Birchbark-covered wigwams
NEIGHBORS: Naskapi, Cree
LIFESTYLE: Hunting
FOOD: Caribou, moose, gathered plant foods, some fish
CRAFTS: Skinwork, birchbark

N

NASKAPI 7:4
LANGUAGE: Algonquian
AREA: Eastern Subarctic
HOUSING: Birchbark-covered wigwams
NEIGHBORS: Montagnais, Cree, Inuit
LIFESTYLE: Hunting, fishing, some gathering
FOOD: Caribou, moose, waterfowl, some gathered plant foods
CRAFTS: Caribou skinwork, birchbark

NATCHEZ (Avoyel) 7:6
LANGUAGE: Natchez
AREA: Southeast
HOUSING: Palisaded townships, thatched cabins on earth mounds
NEIGHBORS: Caddo, Chickasaw, Choctaw
LIFESTYLE: Farming, some hunting
FOOD: Corn, sunflowers, melons, deer, some gathered foods
CRAFTS: Basketry, weaving

NAVAJO (Dine or Dene) 7:9
LANGUAGE: Athapascan
AREA: Southwest
HOUSING: Hogans
NEIGHBORS: Apache, Pueblo
LIFESTYLE: Seminomadic hunting and gathering, herding, farming

FOOD: Small game, gathered roots and berries, corn
CRAFTS: Weaving, silverwork

NEZ PERCÉ (Chute-Pa-Lu) 7:13
LANGUAGE: Penutian
AREA: Plateau
HOUSING: Cattail mat multifamily houses, some tepees
NEIGHBORS: Flathead, Cayuse, Shoshoni
LIFESTYLE: Fishing, hunting, gathering
FOOD: Salmon, buffalo, deer, gathered roots and berries
CRAFTS: Basketry, woven bags, skinwork, beadwork

NOOTKA (Nuu-Chah-Nulth) 7:19
LANGUAGE: Wakashan
AREA: Northwest Coast
HOUSING: Split cedar plank
NEIGHBORS: Coast Salish, Kwakiutl
LIFESTYLE: Sea-mammal hunting, whaling, fishing
FOOD: Seals, whales, salmon, shellfish, roots and berries
CRAFTS: Woodcarving, basketry, some shellwork

O

OJIBWAY (CHIPPEWA; also Saulteaux, Flambeaux, Pillagers, Anishinabe) 7:24
LANGUAGE: Algonquian
AREA: Great Lakes
HOUSING: Large villages of bark-covered wigwams
NEIGHBORS: Cree, Ottawa, Iroquois
LIFESTYLE: Farming, hunting, fishing, gathering
FOOD: Caribou, moose, fish, wild rice, maple syrup, fruits
CRAFTS: Basketry, birchbark, wood-carving, rush weaving

OMAHA
LANGUAGE: Siouan
AREA: Eastern Plains
HOUSING: Earth lodge villages, tepees when hunting
NEIGHBORS: Pawnee, Sioux, Iowa, Oto
LIFESTYLE: Farming, seasonal buffalo hunting
FOOD: Corn, buffalo, deer, gathered plant foods
CRAFTS: Skinwork, beadwork, ribbon appliqué

OSAGE 7:32
LANGUAGE: Siouan
AREA: Eastern Plains
HOUSING: Earth lodge villages, tepees when hunting
NEIGHBORS: Pawnee, Kiowa, Caddo
LIFESTYLE: Farming, seasonal buffalo hunting
FOOD: Corn, buffalo, deer, gathered plant foods
CRAFTS: Skinwork, beadwork, ribbon appliqué

OTO
LANGUAGE: Siouan
AREA: Eastern Plains
HOUSING: Earth lodge villages, tepees when hunting
NEIGHBORS: Pawnee, Osage, Sioux
LIFESTYLE: Farming, seasonal buffalo hunting
FOOD: Corn, buffalo, deer, gathered plant foods
CRAFTS: Skinwork, beadwork

OTTAWA
LANGUAGE: Algonquian
AREA: Great Lakes
HOUSING: Villages of bark-covered wigwams
NEIGHBORS: Ojibway, Cree, Iroquois
LIFESTYLE: Farming, fishing, hunting, gathering
FOOD: Wild rice, fish, game, gathered roots and berries
CRAFTS: Quillwork, birchbark

P

PAIUTE (Chemehuevi) 7:36
LANGUAGE: Uto-Aztecan
AREA: Great Basin
HOUSING: Brush-covered wickiups, some use of tepees
NEIGHBORS: Ute, Shoshoni
LIFESTYLE: Nomadic hunting and gathering
FOOD: Small game, birds, roots and berries, insects, reptiles
CRAFTS: Basketry, rabbitskin blankets

PAPAGO (Tohono-O-Otam) 7:45
LANGUAGE: Uto-Aztecan
AREA: Southwest
HOUSING: Thatched wickiups
NEIGHBORS: Pima, Apache, Mohave
LIFESTYLE: Farming, hunting, gathering, fishing
FOOD: Corn, beans, squash, deer, roots and berries, some fish
CRAFTS: Basketry

PAWNEE (Skidi, Kitkehaxki, Pitahaurata, Chaui) 7:49
LANGUAGE: Caddoan
AREA: Eastern Plains
HOUSING: Earth lodge villages
NEIGHBORS: Sioux, Arapaho, Kiowa, Osage
LIFESTYLE: Farming, seasonal buffalo hunting
FOOD: Corn, beans, squash, buffalo, deer, roots and berries
CRAFTS: Skinwork, beadwork

PEQUOT
LANGUAGE: Algonquian
AREA: Eastern Woodland
HOUSING: Stockaded towns of bark-covered lodges
NEIGHBORS: Northeast Woodland Algonquian
LIFESTYLE: Farming, some hunting and gathering
FOOD: Corn, beans, squash, deer, gathered roots and berries
CRAFTS: Quillwork, beadwork

PIMA (Ah-Kee-Mult-O-O-Tam) 7:45
LANGUAGE: Uto-Aztecan
AREA: Southwest
HOUSING: Thatched wickiups
NEIGHBORS: Papago, Apache, Mohave
LIFESTYLE: Farming, hunting, gathering, fishing
FOOD: Corn, beans, squash, deer, roots, berries, mesquite, fish
CRAFTS: Basketry

POMO 7:60
LANGUAGE: Pomo (Hokan)
AREA: Central California
HOUSING: Tule-covered lodges
NEIGHBORS: Hupa, Wintun, Miwok
LIFESTYLE: Hunting, fishing, gathering
FOOD: Game, fish, acorns, gathered roots and berries
CRAFTS: Basketry, featherwork

PONCA
LANGUAGE: Siouan
AREA: Eastern Plains
HOUSING: Villages of earth lodges, tepees when hunting
NEIGHBORS: Sioux, Pawnee, Omaha
LIFESTYLE: Farming, seasonal buffalo hunting
FOOD: Corn, vegetables, buffalo, deer, gathered roots and berries
CRAFTS: Skinwork, beadwork

POTAWATOMI
LANGUAGE: Algonquian
AREA: Northeast Woodland
HOUSING: Bark-covered lodges
NEIGHBORS: Sauk and Fox, Kickapoo, Iroquois
LIFESTYLE: Farming, fishing, some hunting and gathering
FOOD: Corn, fish, deer, wild plants and roots
CRAFTS: Beadwork, ribbon appliqué, birchbark

POWHATAN Confederacy
LANGUAGE: Algonquian
AREA: Eastern Woodland
HOUSING: Palisaded villages of thatch- or bark-covered lodges
NEIGHBORS: Northeast Woodland Algonquian
LIFESTYLE: Farming, some hunting and gathering
FOOD: Corn, beans, squash, deer, gathered plant foods
CRAFTS: Beadwork

PUEBLO 8:17
LANGUAGE: Tanoan and Keresan
AREA: Southwest
HOUSING: Multistory adobe
NEIGHBORS: Apache, Navajo
LIFESTYLE: Farming, some hunting
FOOD: Corn, beans, squash, deer, gathered roots and berries
CRAFTS: Pottery, silverwork, weaving

S

SALISH 8:57
LANGUAGE: Salishan
AREA: Plateau
HOUSING: Semisubterranean brush- or earth-covered lodges
NEIGHBORS: Blackfoot, Nez Percé, Cayuse
LIFESTYLE: Fishing, hunting, trapping, and gathering
FOOD: Salmon, river fish, deer, wild roots and berries
CRAFTS: Basketry

SAUK and FOX (Sac, Mesquakie) 8:63
LANGUAGE: Algonquian
AREA: Great Lakes
HOUSING: Bark-covered lodges, tepees when hunting
NEIGHBORS: Kickapoo, Sioux
LIFESTYLE: Farming, gathering, trapping, seasonal hunting
FOOD: Corn, beans, squash, wild rice, buffalo, roots and berries
CRAFTS: Quillwork, woven bags, ribbon appliqué

SEMINOLE 9:7
LANGUAGE: Muskogean
AREA: Florida
HOUSING: Palm-thatched chickees raised on stilts
NEIGHBORS: Miccosukee
LIFESTYLE: Fishing, hunting, farming
FOOD: Corn, beans, shellfish, fish, roots
CRAFTS: Ribbon patchwork

SHAWNEE 9:22
LANGUAGE: Algonquian
AREA: Southeast
HOUSING: Palisaded townships
NEIGHBORS: Kickapoo, Creek
LIFESTYLE: Farming, some hunting
FOOD: Corn, deer, gathered roots and berries
CRAFTS: Beadwork, some pottery

SHOSHONI (Tsosoni)
LANGUAGE: Uto-Aztecan
AREA: Western Plains
HOUSING: Brush-covered wickiups, tepees
NEIGHBORS: Blackfoot, Cheyenne, Arapaho, Ute, Paiute
LIFESTYLE: Nomadic hunting and gathering
FOOD: Buffalo in East, wild plant foods in West
CRAFTS: Skinwork, beadwork

SIOUX (Dakota, Lakota, Nakota) 9:27
LANGUAGE: Siouan
AREA: Northern and Eastern Plains
HOUSING: Tepees
NEIGHBORS: Blackfoot, Crow, Cheyenne, Arapaho, Winnebago
LIFESTYLE: Nomadic hunting and gathering
FOOD: Buffalo, deer, wild plants
CRAFTS: Skinwork, beadwork

T

TAOS (Tua) 9:51
LANGUAGE: Tanoan
AREA: Southwest
HOUSING: Multistory adobe
NEIGHBORS: Pueblo tribes, Apache, Navajo
LIFESTYLE: Farming
FOOD: Corn, beans, squash, some game, gathered foods
CRAFTS: Pottery, some basketry

TIMUCUA (Utina) 9:59
LANGUAGE: Timucuan (related to Muskogean)
AREA: Florida
HOUSING: Villages of palm-thatched houses
NEIGHBORS: Calusa, Apalachee
LIFESTYLE: Farming, hunting, fishing
FOOD: Corn, beans, fish, birds, alligators, plant foods
CRAFTS: Pottery

TLINGIT 9:61
LANGUAGE: Tlingit (related to Athapascan)
AREA: Northern Northwest Coast
HOUSING: Split cedar plank
NEIGHBORS: Tsimshian, Chugach, Inuit, Northern Athapascan
LIFESTYLE: Trading, sea-mammal hunting, fishing
FOOD: Salmon, other fish, sea mammals, shellfish
CRAFTS: Woodcarving, basketry, weaving

TSIMSHIAN 10:23
LANGUAGE: Chimmesyan (related to Penutian)
AREA: Northwest Coast
HOUSING: Split cedar plank
NEIGHBORS: Tlingit, Haida, Bella Bella
LIFESTYLE: Trading, sea-mammal hunting, fishing
FOOD: Salmon, other fish, sea mammals, shellfish
CRAFTS: Woodcarving, basketry

U

UTE (Nunt'z)
LANGUAGE: Uto-Aztecan
AREA: Great Basin
HOUSING: Brush-covered wickiups
NEIGHBORS: Paiute, Shoshoni, Navajo
LIFESTYLE: Nomadic gathering
FOOD: Small game, reptiles, insects, plants, roots and berries
CRAFTS: Basketry, beadwork

W

WICHITA
LANGUAGE: Caddoan
AREA: Southern Plains
HOUSING: Domed thatched houses
NEIGHBORS: Kiowa, Comanche, Caddo Confederacy
LIFESTYLE: Farming, hunting

FOOD: Corn, buffalo, deer, gathered roots and berries
CRAFTS: Skinwork, beadwork

WINNEBAGO
LANGUAGE: Siouan
AREA: Great Lakes
HOUSING: Earth- or bark-covered houses, tepees when hunting
NEIGHBORS: Sauk and Fox, Potawatomi
LIFESTYLE: Farming, seasonal hunting
FOOD: Corn, buffalo, deer, wild rice, fish, roots and berries
CRAFTS: Pottery, skin-, quill- and beadwork

WINTUN
LANGUAGE: Wintun (Penutian)
AREA: Central California
HOUSING: Mat-covered lodges
NEIGHBORS: Pomo, Maidu
LIFESTYLE: Hunting, fishing, gathering

FOOD: Salmon, deer, acorns, gathered roots and berries
CRAFTS: Basketry, featherwork, some woodwork

Y

YAQUI
LANGUAGE: Uto-Aztecan
AREA: Southwest
HOUSING: Villages of thatched lodges
NEIGHBORS: Pima, Papago, Apache
LIFESTYLE: Farming, hunting, gathering
FOOD: Corn, small game, gathered roots and berries
CRAFTS: Skinwork, some woodcarving

YUMA (Quechan)
LANGUAGE: Hokan
AREA: Southwest
HOUSING: Thatched lodges
NEIGHBORS: Mohave, Papago, Pima, Apache
LIFESTYLE: Farming, hunting, gathering

FOOD: Corn, melons, deer, gathered roots and berries
CRAFTS: Beadwork, pottery dolls

YUROK (Weitspekan)
LANGUAGE: Yurok
AREA: Northern California
HOUSING: Driftwood or plank
NEIGHBORS: Klamath, Karok, Modoc
LIFESTYLE: Hunting, fishing, gathering
FOOD: Deer, fish, roots and berries
CRAFTS: Shellwork, basketry

Z

ZUNI (A'shiwi) 10:62
LANGUAGE: Zunian
AREA: Southwest
HOUSING: Multistory adobe
NEIGHBORS: Pueblo, Apache, Navajo
LIFESTYLE: Farming, some hunting
FOOD: Corn, beans, squash, small game, some gathered plants
CRAFTS: Pottery, weaving, woodcarving, silverwork

FURTHER READING

Calloway, C. G. *New Worlds for All: Indians, Europeans, and the Remaking of Early America.* Baltimore, MD: Johns Hopkins University Press, 1997.

Edmonds, S. and P. Kernaghan. *Native Peoples of North America: Diversity and Development.* New York: Cambridge University Press, 1994.

Hirschfelder, A., ed. *Nature Heritage: Personal Accounts by American Indians, 1790 to the Present.* New York: Macmillan, General Reference, 1995.

Hoxie, F. E. *Encyclopedia of North American Indians.* Boston, MA: Houghton Mifflin Co., 1996.

Hyslop, S. G. and H. Woodhead, eds. *Chroniclers of Indian Life.* Alexandria, VA: Time Life, 1996.

Johnson, M. G. and R. Hook. *The Native Tribes of North America: A Concise Encyclopedia.* New York: Macmillan, 1994.

Josephy, A. M. *500 Nations: An Illustrated History of North American Indians.* New York: Knopf, 1998.

Keller, R. H. and M. F. Turek. *American Indians and National Parks.* Tuscon, AZ: University of Arizona Press, 1998.

Long, A. and M. Boldt. *Governments in Conflict: Provinces and Indian Nations in Canada.* Toronto, Ontario: University of Toronto Press, 1998.

Maynard, J., ed. *Through Indian Eyes: The Untold Story of Native American Peoples.* Pleasantville, NY: Readers Digest, 1996.

Meltzer, D. J. *Search for the First Americans.* Washington, DC: Smithsonian Books, 1995.

Miller, L., ed. *From the Heart: Voices of the American Indian.* New York: Knopf, 1995.

Nichols, R. L. *Indians in the United States and Canada: A Comparative History.* Lincoln, NE: University of Nebraska Press, 1998.

Pritzker, B. *Native Americans: An Encyclopedia of History, Culture, and Peoples.* Santa Barbara, CA: ABC-Clio, 1998.

Sperber, C. and A. J. Joffe. *The First Immigrants from Asia: A Population History of the North American Indians.* New York: Plenum Publishing Corporation, 1992.

Steele, I. K. *Warpaths: Invasions of North America.* New York: Oxford University Press, 1994.

Thornton, R., ed. *Studying Native America: Problems and Prospects.* Madison, WI: University of Wisconsin Press, 1999.

Trigger, B. G. and W. E. Washburn, eds. *The Cambridge History of the Native Peoples of the Americas: North America.* New York: Cambridge University Press, 1996.

Turner, G. *Indians of North America.* New York: Sterling Publications, 1992.

Waldrum, C. and M. Braun. *Atlas of the North American Indian.* New York: Facts on File, 1995.

Warhus, M. *Another America: Native American Maps and the History of Our Land.* New York: St. Martin's Press, 1997.

SET INDEX

Volume numbers and page numbers for main entries are shown in **bold**. Page numbers of illustrations or picture captions are shown in *italic*. Additional references can be found in the SEE ALSOS at the ends of the main entries.

ACKNOWLEDGMENTS

Picture Credits

Corbis: 9, 43, Bettmann 17, Tim Thompson 55, Peter Wilson 52; Kobal Collection: 58, 59; Northwind Picture Archive: 23, 35, 53; Peter Newark Historical Pictures: 5, 6, 25, 26, 27, 28, 34, 37, 45, 56, 57, 60–61, 62; N. J. Saunders 41; Sylvia Bancroft Hunt Pictures: 4, 8, 19, 24, 29, 30, 31, 33, 38, 49, 50, 51, 54, 64; Werner Forman Archive: 12t, A. Sponr Collection, Plains Indian Museum 18, Ed Merrin Collection 12b, Field Museum of Natural History 32, 40b, Glenbow Museum, Canada 22, L. Larom Collection, Plains Indian Museum 21, Maxell Museum of Anthropology 48, Museum of the American Indian, Heye Foundation 39, 40t, National Museum of Anthropology 11, 15t, 16, Private Collection 14, Private Collection, NY 15b, Provincial Museum, Canada 13, Willoughby Howard Collection, Plains Indian Museum 20.

Text Contributors

Norman Bancroft Hunt, Steven L. Grafe, Ray Granger, Jen Green, Charlotte Greig, Casey Horton, Chris Marshall, Nigel Ritchie, Antony Shaw, Stephen Small, Donald Sommerville, Chris Westhorp.